MODERN WITCH'S
Book of
SYMBOLS

MODERN WITCH'S
Book of
SYMBOLS

Sarah Lyddon Morrison

BOXTREE

First published 1997 by Citadel Press, New Jersey

First published in Great Britain 1998 by Boxtree
an imprint of Macmillan Publishers Ltd
25 Eccleston Place, London SW1W 9NF
and Basingstoke

Associated companies throughout the world

ISBN 0 7522 2109 4

1 3 5 7 9 8 6 4 2

A CIP catalogue record for this book is available from
the British Library

Phototypeset by Intype London Ltd
Printed and bound in Great Britain by
Mackays of Chatham plc, Chatham, Kent

To James Earl Butler
Companion and Inspiration

CONTENTS

O

Oak Tree, Owl
97–98

P

Peace Sign, Pearl, Pentacle, Phoenix, Pigs, Pilgrims, Pomegranate,
Prehistoric Symbols, Priesthood, Propaganda, Pyramid
99–112

Q R

Queen, Quadriga, Raven, Rebirth, Red, Renaissance Painters,
Rigveda, Rose
113–120

S

Scales, Second Coming, Seven, Sex, Sickle, Silver and Gold,
Skull, Sphinx, Stairs, Star, Stone Worship, Stork, Sun,
Swastika, Symbolist Poets
121–139

T

Tarot, Temples, Three, Tortoise, Tree of Life, Triangle, Trident,
Trisula, Two Principles
141–155

U V

Unicorn, Virgin Mary, Vishnu, Vowels
157–164

W

Water, Wheel, White Horse, Wisdom
165–168

X Y Z

Xanthippe Yellow, Yoni, Yoke, Zodiac
169–171

Bibliography

INTRODUCTION

Symbol is a word taken from the Greek which means "recognition system." Unless properly understood, all symbols seem like a magician's work. A symbol is something that suggests or stands for something else, like a lion being a symbol of courage. Their meanings aren't often automatically apparent. In many cases, symbols require interpretation before we can understand them. For example, if you didn't know that a fish was the symbol of the early Christians, you might not know that your friend was a Christian unless he told you what the silver fish pin on his jacket represented.

Symbols appear everywhere in our everyday lives and are integral to our culture. Symbols are common throughout Western literature; the French even had Symbolist poets. I can well recall my college days when I had to interpret the symbolism in poetry or books (*Moby Dick!*).

In this book I explain everyday symbols and many that are more esoteric. You'll find a sort of crossbreeding of symbology, presented alphabetically, which is meant to indicate how wide and deep the subject is.

I want to convey here the importance of symbols in our lives. For the modern witch, specifically, knowledge of symbols can broaden the scope of their occult knowledge.

Good luck with your occult studies.

A

ALCHEMISTS

The Sphinx is a riddle to man's deepest consciousness. It's a blank face that titillates us most. The key is the mind, and that is man's mystery.

The ancient world based its intellectuality in analogies much different from those we use today. The dream of old was to call on the gods and have them appear. Today we have an entirely different intellectual system than the ancients had. Today's scientists desire to reduce matter to its smallest particles. Psychologists, today, accept fragmentary symbols working toward the end of understanding the emotions. Repressed emotion is what they look for in these symbols.

We have called the old systems, which believed in the constellation myths for their symbolism, magic, and astrology.

In modern times we go back to the ancients' system of thought for sustenance. Man's desire for knowledge slips back to the world of dreams which began in the nineteenth century with Shelly, Coleridge, and Wordsworth. In these poets, the hidden soul was the subject of much seeking. The association of images was strong in Shakespeare as well as William Blake. Some think these poets dreamed of things to come. Symbolism brought these poets to glory and set the pattern of the universe for them.

The poets brought to life the moral injustices that occurred when the heavens and man intermingled. The astrologers read life in the stars according to a man's hour of birth. The alchemists who sought for a soul in matter of all kinds (and to transform base metals into gold) did so with astrology, the use of which was to define the transmutation of the soul of man by image, figure, and correspondence through philosophical chemistry.

The alchemists tried to find a path through the jungles of the mind – and they were followed by today's psychologists. The alchemists were secretive and hid their writings from untrained eyes. So perplexing are those writings still extant that it is difficult to follow their work. But enough can be understood to interest us – the history of psychology, the study of myths, and the examination of dreams all require a universal system of symbols.

In the sixteenth and seventeenth centuries – which were Platonist times – an attempt was made to bring together Platonic and Aristotelian thought and philosophy. The attempt brought the myths of the classic period into line with the tradition of folklore, making them a whole pattern of thought. Now much of that thought is lost to us. Secrecy prohibited the philosophy, religious, and political upheavals. But people who were magicians and mystics let their imaginations run free in hidden societies. Cosmogonic theories were born in secrecy, and symbolism flourished. These people were cabalists, Rosicrucians, astrologers, and alchemists.

The old cosmology and thinkers are no longer revered, for their symbolic system was theological, and their physical investigations were much the same as those of our scientists. So the triumph of the scientists broke down the classic patterns of thought. Now alchemy is regarded with no respect, even though it was based on two thousand years of practical theory. And the artworks produced in its name have, like classic thought, gone to the back burner of artistic endeavor.

Symbols are a part of man's deepest self – the eternal in him. In theology of old and psychology of new, symbols had to do with states of mind and modes of emotions; the stars and their patterns were the great mind of God. The study of dreams shows the symbolism in determining thought in consciousness – as it was useful in unfolding the thought of the imagination.

According to the astrologers, a birth was related to the whole universe as of the moment in time in which the person was born. The first recorders of myths had the understanding of the astrologers. There was, they believed, a relationship between modes and the mind's capability of producing symbols which in astrology related to the position of the sun and stars.

Man has set the mind's symbology in the stars, but his phantasms and his symbols are intensely different.

The most profound thinkers of the day studied signs and symbols. In those times, there was a burgeoning of artists and symbolic thought that has never been seen again. Our Western literature was founded by the dreamers who thought deeply about myth and religion. The humanists, meanwhile, read the Cabala and astrology for the soul of the world. They believed in secret influences at work touching the lives of man. For two thousand years the universe of men and women reigned.

In Paradise there was Adam and Eve and the serpent – the dragon – who was responsible for the fall of man.

The conquest of the dragon comes in the Bible in St. John's Apocalypse. Puritans and Protestants upheld the myth because it symbolically seemed to show the end of Catholicism and Rome (the scarlet whore of Babylon).

A lot of the misunderstanding of symbols has to do with astrology, which is thought by many to be a mere foreteller of events. But in ancient times, telling of the future was just an astrological sideline: the science of astrology was much more – the knowledge and secrets of the stars. The ancients thought that man's soul was as old as the universe itself. It descended through time and space to earth. The faculty of making images (symbols, too) is employed by mankind for his understanding.

By use of a symbol, the mind is focused on an application. Wide psychological experience is required to understand many symbols. A symbol is an interpretive medium between the outside world and the inner world. Symbols are useless to those with materialistic minds, but symbols represent a direct path to knowledge to the mind that understands associations.

Alchemy last affected thought in the seventeenth century when the zodiac of the alchemist was different than that of the astrologer.

At the time of Shakespeare, astrologers were predicting people's entire lives at the time of their births. There were people who secretly studied and guarded the ancient theories concerning the outer universe of stars as reflected in a man's life. Within this group was another, the alchemists, who used a similar order of signs and symbols of great mystery and who dealt with the inner psychological life. Alchemists believed that the planets in the spheres were in the same order as the seven metals of earth.

The Alchemists believed that man was a microcosm of the universe – and all things in the system dwell in him. The alchemists believed that there could be redemption from a fallen state of the mind through a return to its origin in a re-integrating of the chemistry of the soul. They also believed in the perfectibility of the soul.

The soul traversing the realm of time was traced by the astrologer through the stars and gases of heaven through the planets and constellations set in the mind, so that the kingdom that is lost could be found again. The speculation of the astrologer would never have found acceptance. But the thought pattern and analogies were beautiful, perhaps unscientific but artistic and imaginative.

The alchemists and astrologers were seers, and they studied the dream life. Heaven was a dream for those who conquered hell. Alchemists – the precursors of chemists – were the passionate knowledge seekers in the depth of man's mind.

The constellations of the zodiac were in a lunar-solar pathway. A correspondence arose in the naming of these groups of stars between the universal and the personal, which in turn displayed a psychological resonance – a connection between the stellar and the mundane.

Man saw himself patterned after God, and what man saw in the skies reflected his thought; he related the movement of the stars to his moods and passions. He saw in the heavens the movement of the minds of the world. In this world, mind was the past and the future, and some thought these could be read in the stars.

ANCIENT ANIMAL DRAWINGS

Drawings of birds, elephants, boars, bulls, and serpents can be found on the walls of caves in ancient Britain. Many early people "drew" their religion with symbols. Besides these small symbols, we have the great temples such as Stonehenge, Woodhenge, and Avebury and Stennos in the Orkneys, Tara in Ireland, and Callenish in the Hebrides. All are prehistoric, and all are important to the culture.

ANEMONE

As the Greek myth has it, when a wild boar killed her lover Adonis, Venus changed the blood from his wound into an anemone. The wind blows anemone blossoms away very quickly, which symbolizes the short life of Adonis. Symbolic of sorrow and death, the Arabs refer to the anemone as "darling" – their name for the Greek Adonis.

Adonis was mourned at the Phoenician sanctuary at Byblos, and it was said that his blood flowed in the river each Easter. The women there rejoiced at this sign of his resurrection. Today, near the valley of Jebeil, which is near Beirut, the red earth in springtime washes down the hillsides and covers them with blood – red dirt which tinges the anemones that grow there.

In the ancient days of Christianity, the anemone, which has tripartite leaves, symbolized the Holy Trinity. Anemone flowers were said to appear on Calvary after Christ's death there. Like Venus, the Virgin Mary has been painted bearing the anemone as a sign of her great sorrow.

ANIMALS, CHRISTIAN

The animal symbols of Christianity come from the distant past and their sources are mystery religions – for example, witchcraft and sorcery. They all symbolize the dichotomy of man and God. Man is an animal, but he has a soul or spirit as well, and so is two-fold. Animals represent the animal nature of man.

Animals sometimes represent God, sometimes evil. The universality of the struggle between God and Satan expands with Ezekiel's Apocalypse. Man is symbolized by angel, lion, bull, and eagle, becoming a sphinx. This animal can represent vision and purity, or sins such as gluttony.

Pelicans are sometimes depicted on the top of the crucifix where it reads INRI. The adult bird is cutting his breast for blood to feed his offspring. The symbol is Christ's blood shed for the world. This sacrifice restores the spiritual life.

Bulls symbolize the sacrifice through blood; also fertility, due to his powerful generative capacity. The bull is one of the four apocalyptic animals in the vision of Ezekiel and St. John.

Boars were considered spiritual by the Druids. In Christianity, the wild boar has usually symbolized the Antichrist. They symbolize anger and are in opposition to the dove and the lamb (symbols of Christ).

Lions were animals worshipped by the Persian Mithras. The divine Mithras was pictured as a god with a lion's head and a human body. The heraldic lion of the Persian state was a lion with a man's head and a sun on his back. This symbolized the worship of Mithras.

Christ is represented, sometimes, as a man with angel's wings. He symbolized the perfect human.

Satan is often depicted with wings too, but they are usually bat wings, and he carries the signs of evil – horns on his head, goat's feet, and a monkey's tail. Sometimes, to represent his complete fall from divinity, the devil takes on the form of an animal with no human characteristics whatever. He was symbolized as a vampire, a snake, and a goat, to name just a few.

Eagle: Christ often took the form of an eagle in early Christian depictions. The eagle is a high flier and predator of extraordinary power. The picture of Christ as an eagle shows him with a shield which denotes honor, thus symbolizing the invulnerability of Christ.

Fish: The fish as a symbol of plenty rises from the Bible story in which Christ shares the loaves and fishes with the multitude. The fish is a symbol of the Christian faith. It also symbolizes Christ.

Animal sacrifices are common in the Old Testament. The calf symbolizes Christ, a virgin among humans, who dies for us all. Calves had to be perfect in order to be offered for sacrifice.

The ram is a leftover symbol from primitive times. It symbolized the god of the hearth to the Gauls.

Goats (especially male ones) symbolize virility and overwhelming sexual desires. Goats have a foul odor which represents depravity. Inner beauty in humans leaves a perfumed scent, while corruption and sin leave evil aromas.

The female goat fares better. She climbs rocky mountains and sees vistas below her in detail. She symbolizes the gaze of Christ, who sees all.

Dragons were accursed to the Hebrews and in St. John's Apocalypse. In the Middle Ages, a good dragon was born to fight off the evil ones. In Middle Ages' heraldry, the dragon represented vigilance and charity.

Phoenix: Jesus was symbolized as a phoenix because both had miraculous births. The phoenix legend says that the bird builds a fire when it realizes it will soon die, and burns itself up. Out of the ashes comes a new phoenix which embalms the father's ashes in a myrrh egg and flies them to the temple of the sun. The phoenix symbolizes eternity and resurrection.

Owl: Sleeping during the day has brought the owl the symbolic representation of ignorance. The owl has been symbolized as the Jew who didn't recognize Christ in his new body during the resurrection cycle.

Ibis: The Ibis eats flesh and symbolized, for Middle Age Christians, gluttony and sexual knowledge. The Egyptians, on the other hand, regarded the Ibis as purifying – since it ate what it killed. Thus the Ibis came to symbolize resurrection and the guidance of souls to Heaven.

Dove: Doves symbolize the divinity which inspires humans to choose good action instead of evil.

Swallows: They bring fine weather conditions and there-fore symbolize hope. For early Christians they represented hope which descends from Heaven and Christ.

Nightingale: These birds choose to sing in beautiful gar-dens at night. Its song is louder at daybreak with the sun's coming. It symbolizes Christ at Gethsemane sojourning with His disciples through the night.

Crane: A symbol of Christ as he watches over good and evil in combat.

Swan: Christ is a swan in the divine heavens and is drawn to the soul who calls out for Him. A swan bearing a cross is the symbol of Christ bearing his own crucifix.

Hen: The black hen is a symbol of evil. The white hen symbolized Christ; His chicks call to Him like souls longing for Heaven.

ANKH

An Egyptian symbol that stands for life and for life after death. The gods that favored humans were often depicted carrying the ankh by its oval loop. It was carried by dieties and kings who lived in the Hall of Judgment. It's found in Egyptian tomb paintings and has also been found on ancient Christian tombstones in the Nile Valley.

It recently became a popular piece of jewelry. In New York, I, and everyone I know, wore the ankh for fertility.

It was said to have the power of restoring life to those who were dead.

The ankh has been found in Palestine, Phoenicia, and Africa on carved reliefs, tombs, jew-elry, and coins. There is an ankh from Easter Island kept in the British Museum. The ankh was inscribed on the garments of early Christian priests.

APPLE

The apple symbolizes dispute, love, and desire. Although some scholars say that apples grew in the wilderness during the days of Solomon, the apple as we know it didn't grow in ancient times. The fruit designated as an apple was more likely an apricot or a quince.

In Latin, the apple was known as evil. It is commonly thought that the apple was the fruit found on the Tree of Knowledge in the Garden of Eden, but the Bible doesn't actually name it. Nevertheless, by association with original sin, the apple in some cases symbolizes evil.

The round shape of the apple suggests a circle and is therefore symbolic of immortality and the wholeness of the spirituality of man.

The golden apples in the mythology of Greece were tasted by the gods to renew their youth. But the apples of Sodom on the Dead Sea were evil and brought disappointment and disillusion.

References to the mixture of the good and the evil in apples shows up in classic literary references. The Talmud mentions that the apple brings good health ("an apple a day keeps the doctor away") and symbolizes immortality. The apple written of in Arabian Nights cured all ills. Snow White's apple was poisoned and brought deep sleep. In the Psalms the apple is sweet and brings delight. New Testament references to the apple associate it with Christ and make it a symbol of goodness and eternal life.

ARROW

Especially before the invention of gunpowder, the arrow symbolized speed. It was also an emblem of love – which could be sudden as an arrow shot. The Greek god Eros carried a bow and arrows to smite humans with love; a heart shot through with an arrow is still a common symbol of love. Just as quickly as love comes, so may come death, which is sometimes symbolized by a skeleton with an arrow.

ARYANS AND SNAKES

The Aryans, sometimes known as the Sumerians, lived on Mt. Meru in the Sumeru mountain range.

The ancient Aryan religion has developed into Hindu, whose authority is the Sanskrit *Rig Veda*, as perhaps the most ancient books in the world. The Vedas refer to material much older than the books themselves. The *Artharva Veda* predates even the *Rig Veda*. Included in both are details of ritual, much of which is still practiced in present times. The *Artharva Veda* contains a description of the Chakra, a symbol found in British history.

During the Bronze Age, Hindus dominated much of the world. Accounts of those times were entrusted to scientifically trained bards with vast memories. And so the histories were passed along until Sanskrit literature clothed them in the garb of mythology. Some Aryan beliefs traveled to America in the form of shamanism, and Aryans also left their imprint in the legends of the Celts.

If you follow the anthropological tracks across the Bering Strait from Asia to America and thence to Britain as some scholars do, you will find obvious Indo-Celtic affinity. Bali is king of the Netherworld. Britain is sometimes called the Island of Bali or God of Night. Bali sometimes appears as Moon-god. The moon-god married Tara – and their son, Budh, is the planet Mercury.

In the *Ramayama* there are tales of a visit in the Netherworld, and that Daityas and serpents lived in gorgeous cities – and this was all in North America!

The Diatyas were very tall, as were the Fomoricas of the British Isles. These tribes were closely associated with serpents.

Ravana, King of Lanka, took with him on a military journey his general, Prahanta, and he carried a serpent standard. Serpents were significant symbols throughout ancient history.

The *Ramayana* speaks of how the Rakshas under King Ravana found their way to the Netherworld. King Ravana had brought the serpents under subjugation. Tesha of India is also a king – or deity – of the Netherworld serpents, and some scholars think that Tesha was the forerunner of the Shoshonee tribe (the Snake tribes) of the North American continent.

For many centuries, the Antipodes, America, was occupied by Aryans, who traveled to Britain from there.

The Horned Serpent was a god of the Muskogean Confederacy in America. Among its descendants were the Choctaw, Cherokee, and Creeks. The Creeks had a fire ceremony which was called *Pushtika*, a word possibly derived from the Sanskrit syllables.

Many American Indian mounds are shaped in the form of a serpent. It does seem possible that the Aztecs took their name from the Atiks of India.

ASTROLOGICAL SYMBOLS

The sun relates to male and female life activities, to work, honors, achievement, morals, and emotions.

Midheaven relates to attainment, opportunity, and self-expression. It is a doorway to expression, and the male sun and female moon come in and out of it.

The Ascendant relates to the physical body and health.

The planets are well known to many of us. Mercury symbolizes the intellect and thought. Venus represents the affections and artistry as well as social intercourse and cooperation. Mars symbolizes action, enterprise, and tendencies that may lead to quarrels as well as accidents and illness. Jupiter symbolizes prosperity, well-being, and religion. Saturn represents power of organization and construction – on the negative side it lessens desires. Uranus symbolizes violent changes in plans and action, crazy ideas, and a tendency to act in strange ways that may be good or bad. Neptune symbolizes retirement or concealment. It represents long illness, such as cancer, and is connected to death.

In creating a chart, the influence of the planets don't act alone. Venus in the house of Pisces, for example, symbolizes speaking. Mars could pass into Gemini through Pisces and lead the individual into creative endeavors in writing or thought.

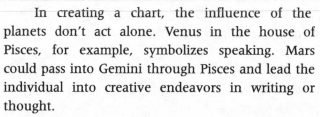

In astrology, marriage is a subject of great interest. If the Sun is found configured with Saturn in a female's chart, no marriage can be predicted for that woman, and likewise in a male's chart which contains the moon configured with Saturn.

When you are reading a fortune, you should never foretell death if you or the person you're doing the reading for is afraid of dying. Even the most sensitive reader is incorrect occasionally.

ATLANTIS
The fabled land of Atlantis was a grand island situated in the Atlantic Ocean between America and Europe. It is said to have been overwhelmed by the sea some ninety-six hundred years before Christ. At the time of the sinking of Atlantis, the Greeks and the Atlanteans were at war – and the Grecian army there died in the upheaval. The poet and historian Solon of Athens (c. 630–c. 560 B.C.) is said to have heard the story of Atlantis while he was traveling in Egypt and to have passed it on to Plato.

One of the best-known accounts of the disaster is in the Troano Manuscript – a Mayan document miraculously left untouched by the Spanish. (There is evidence that some of the Mayan language derived from Greek.) The Troano Manuscript says that sixty-four million inhabitants died when Atlantis went under, in the aftermath of violent earthquakes.

A second document referring to Atlantis was found intact in the lintel of a door in Chichen, a major Mayan city. A third document outlining the disaster is called the Codex Cortesianus, in which Atlantis is referred to as Mu. The flooding of Atlantis before it submerged is thought to be the basis for the story of the Great Flood in the Bible.

AZURE

Azur is the color of the sky where the gods hold forth. Zeus and Odin abode there, and the Virgin Mary is frequently depicted wearing blue robes. Coats of arms carry azure, especially those born by sectors of the Catholic Church. Azure blue is the insignia color of royalty; Swedish, English, and French kings all took azure as their color. One term linking azure and royalty is "blue blood."

In ancient days, blue was the color of divine wisdom, truth, and faith. The sea is azure. "The blues" and "feeling blue" are another association with the color. And light blue is the color assigned to newborn boys.

B

BEANS

Since beans were connected to spirits and ghosts, it was forbidden to eat them in ancient Greece and Rome. The bean was sacred to the goddess Demeter, who gave the Greeks permission to plant every grain and vegetable but beans.

The plant grows in a spiral, so was associated with resurrection. It was thought that errant spirits entered the spiral and were returned as humans. Pythagoras forbade the eating or use of beans by his students; the latter proscription meant they could not vote, as votes were cast by throwing beans into a helmet.

In the first century A.D., Pliny wrote that the souls of the dead lived in beans, and therefore the best charm against ghosts was to throw a bean at them – giving the ghost a chance to go back into the bean.

The Romans were especially tormented by Lemures – mischievous spirits – who returned to cause trouble for the living. To drive them away from the house the father was to wake in the middle of the night on May 9, 11, or 13, snap his fingers, and wash his hands three times. Then he was to fill his lips with black beans and spit them out behind him saying, "I throw away these beans and bring back my family to myself."

BEES

From the earliest days of Egyptian rule, the bee has been a symbol of industriousness and order. The beehive is a marvel of organization. Legend has it that Jupiter was once fed by the bees and that Plato's gift for writing and philosophy came from a bee that touched his mouth when he was an infant in his cradle.

In ancient times the city of Athens was famous for its honey, and some said that the temple at Delphi was built by bees.

Virgil said that new methods of beekeeping were taught to the Greeks by Aristaeus. When his hive died, his mother, Cyrens the nymph, told him to make a sacrifice of four bulls and four heifers, and to leave the bodies on the altar for nine days. In the legend, bees emerged from the bodies to form new swarms.

Human souls were said to travel in beelike swarms and to fly toward Heaven as a group. Mohammed even allowed the bee to become part of the Moslem paradise because of the legend of the swarming souls.

St. Ambrose compared the Church to a beehive, and a Christian working hard for the Church to a worker bee.

It was said of witches that if a queen bee was swallowed by the witch it would help her overcome trials and tortures and keep silent about the Craft.

BIBLICAL SYMBOLS

Names are important in Biblical symbolism. They represent the person's personality and character. A change in name can signify a change in character. Saul became Paul when he renounced his life before meeting Christ, for example. *Jesse,* David's father's name, means *God Exists.*

When you read the Bible symbolically, the text can take on new meaning. For example, *Jesus* means *God Saver.* This symbolic and most fitting name was given to him at birth. *Elijah* means *God Himself.* When the Bible says that Elijah appeared, it's the same as saying God appeared. It's unfortunate that many people don't have a knowledge of Hebrew to help them interpret the meanings of the names and other elements of Bible stories. *Egypt,* for example, means *bondage,* and *Eden* means *delight.*

On occasion, the Bible employs words that are figurative, not literal. *Land,* for example, may mean *consciousness,* the only reality, referring to various levels of awareness in a human being. The direction *east* may mean those areas of consciousness within one; *west* may mean outside. *North,* being "above," may refer to the conscious mind, and *south* to the subcon-

scious. All the directions taken together refer to the harmony
of consciousness.

Consciousness and *Land* are sometimes interchangeable
concepts in the Bible. Words such as *wilderness, mountains,* and
valleys may symbolize states of consciousness.

For example, God told Abraham to raise up his eyes and
look in all directions and that God would give Abraham all
that he saw. Since this was symbolic *land,* God was saying that
He would help Abraham achieve a perspective that was like
His own. What Abraham believed in was his.

Jesus prayed in the wilderness. He spent His time in
meditation and communion with God. He gave His Sermon
on the Mount after deep spiritual communication with
God.

Beulah Land, the place prepared for the children of Israel,
is symbolic too. It means oneness with God. *Beulah* means
married and *Beulah Land* means perfect marriage with God.

The biblical word *house* may mean consciousness of mind,
body, and daily duties. Our souls live in that house. The house
of morning and the house of prayer refer to states that we
attain to in our conscious lives. To live in the House of the
Lord is to attain oneness with our Creator.

To *eat* symbolizes the taking in of conscious experience. *Water* represents the fluid quality of thought. *Heaven*
is the state of being of ideas, the conscious awareness of
God. The concept of *as in Heaven, so on Earth* means as it is
within, so be it without; the thoughts of the mind made
manifest in the world.

The Bible contains mystic numbers which are a key to
understanding the symbolism of the Bible.

Seven is the most common mystical number appearing in
the Bible. It means perfection in its symbolic form. That's why
God gave note to the seven days of His work of creation. He
rested on the seventh day. This is the completion meant by the
symbolic seven. Our consciousness is supposed to be at rest on
the seventh day.

The number *twelve* is also a symbolic number in the Bible. It represents spiritual fulfillment. Seven symbolizes the fulfillment of the mind, but twelve is spiritual perfection.

Some of the twelves mystically used in the Bible are the twelve tribes of Israel, twelve disciples, and the twelve pillars. The twelve disciples named also symbolize the spiritual faculties in man. The fish that Jesus gave to the multitude were in twelve baskets. These are the bread of life, or Word of God.

In Revelation there are twelve stars as God's fulfillment through illumination and twelve angels as messengers of God or, again, our spiritual thought processes. There are twelve foundations to the new Jerusalem.

The number *forty* is perhaps the most mystical number in the Bible. Forty symbolizes a completed amount of time, stages of spiritual growth.

Moses spent forty days and forty nights on the mountain. He was in meditation throughout this period and close to God. Elijah spent forty days and forty nights on Mt. Horeb and, again, on Mt. Carmel. The Israelites were in the hand of the Philistines for forty years. Jesus Himself was in the wilderness forty days and forty nights.

BLACK

Black is the color of night and has a connotation of being bad – the opposite of daylight. Black stands for fear, death, misfortune. The Underworld is depicted as black, just as Heaven is light. Gods associated with night and black are Hecate, Ceres, and Pluto. Hell is often depicted as black with flames shooting forth. The Devil in occult ceremonies is depicted in the Black Mass with black animals – especially the black cat. Black is also the color of mourning, and is associated with depression. In some churches robes and other articles of dress are black, to remind worshippers of death and the sins of the living.

BLOOD

Blood is a powerful symbol of life, a vital force and an offering for the gods. In ancient times, sacrifices of milk or honey were sometimes substituted for blood, which was the most precious sacrifice of all. The ancients sacrificed animals to ward off pain and evil, and of course the greatest blood sacrifice of all time was Christ's own sacrifice of self for sin.

In alchemy, blood was used to create the Stone, as it was full of the energy of life. And in the Catholic mass today, the bread and wine are transformed into Christ's blood and body.

In France, the people watching the execution of Louis XVI tried to get some blood from the body. They dipped their handkerchiefs in it and used it as an amulet against disease and evil. The Greeks thought they could revitalize themselves by drinking the blood of a dead gladiator. It is believed even today that the blood of an executed man – if he was vital and in good health – protects one from all misfortunes.

Blood is red and the color is symbolic of passion, violence, and danger. Mars was the Roman god of war and bloodshed and in astrology.

BLUE

The color blue symbolizes celestial gods and goddesses. The Greek god Zeus wore blue robes, as did the Roman Jupiter and Juno, his wife. Odin of Scandinavia wore blue and, with the advent of Christianity, the Virgin Mary wore blue.

The colors of St. Andrew, as patron saint of Scotland, are blue and silver, with the cross in a background of blue.

Blue was present on a variety of coats of arms – especially in France. The government of France chose the symbol of lilies on a blue-and-gold background to represent itself. A purple-blue (now known as royal blue) was the symbol of royalty. This color was worn by kings of France, England, and Sweden. Sashes worn by royalty were blue and the British Order of Garter is blue. The Cordon Bleu of France came from the blue ribbon or sash worn by royalty. Blue is the color favored by conservatives in England.

In ancient times, blue stood for divine wisdom. In the church it became the color of faith. It symbolizes fidelity, honesty, and innocence. People attracted to blue are unselfish, hopeful, religious, and kind, with a pronounced interest in the occult.

BOAR

The wild boar, which can be found today throughout the British Isles, is the symbol of St. Andrew. Wearing the coat of arms of St. Andrew, Fife – who is the patron saint of Scotland – is shown with a cross of St. Andrew in the background. Below this cross is a tree and a boar – both Aryan symbols.

Boars are carved in rock or stone and in hog-backed gravestones. One stone at Knock-na-Gael is inscribed with a boar and there is another in Argyle where the first Scottish King was crowned.

Near the Shrine of St. Andrew is St. David's cathedral in Southern Wales. On it is carved a boar that is associated with the saint.

According to legend, a wild boar once stole a child and became its parent. When the real parents got their child back they named him Andrew, because of the association of the boar with St. Andrew. The MacAndrews family claims descent from the child of this myth.

In ancient Cornish, the word for *boar* is Bora. Is it possible that the word traveled to the Pacific as Bora Bora?

In India the boar is regarded as a symbol of fertility because the boar was the first "farmer" to plow. He plowed the land with his tusks while searching for roots, which prepared the land for seeding. Thus the boar became the symbol of one pre-Christian fertility cult. Ground so plowed may be regarded as both a mental and physical symbol; the soils of both mind and body must be plowed and seeded to maximize growth.

BOWL

It's often not the bowl itself, but what it contains that is symbolic. Offerings of bowls of fruit or honey were part of the sacraments of the Greeks and Romans. Hygea, the Greek goddess of health, carried a bowl that symbolized gifts to the gods. She still sometimes shows up on drugstore signs. A bowl is often found on Jewish gravestones and in the catacombs that date from the earliest days of Christianity.

Water symbolized life and was often offered in jugs. It was the sign of fertility, regeneration, salvation, and eternal life. The jug symbolized great waters – Euphrates, Tigris, Nile, and Tiber Rivers. Oceanus, the ocean god, was depicted with a water jug. Mary Magdalene carried an anointing jug to Jesus, from which she poured oil to bathe his feet.

BULL

Ptah, Egypt's Creation god, was worshipped in the form of a bull as Apis or Hopi. He was also joined by another bull named Kanobus, whose name translates to "the Great Sun." A third bull worshipped was Bakis or "the Great Light" – or to the Greeks, Bacchus. The Egyptian Creator was also symbolized by a fourth bull named Ur-Mer. *Ur* meant fire to the Semites and is also related to Mer, the Assyrian god of Lightning. The Great Bull of early Europe was the light of the fire and was named Horus – the Egyptian Apollo. The cult of Horus was so great in Egypt that mention of his name signified God.

There is a temple in China dedicated to the bull, and similar worship was to be found in Japan and Hindustan.

Thor, the Scandinavian Jupiter, was symbolized at some temples with a bull's head and the ancient languages there represented the bull as the sun.

C

CABALA

The symbolism of numbers is emphasized in the Cabala, which employs a system of numeric interpretation. In the cult of Cabala called Gematria, the number of letters reveal meanings in the Bible. One example is: Adding together the numerical value of the first and second words of Genesis results in the number 1116, which is the numerical value of the Hebrew words: "In the beginning of the year it was created." This sentence can be interpreted to mean that God created the world in the fall season. Another example is that the Jewish letter *A* shows up six times in the first and last verses of the Jewish Bible and means (according to the Cabala) that the span from the beginning to the ending of the world will be six thousand years.

Reading Cabala was all the rage among scholars in the Middle Ages, who believed that the Cabala had been passed down by the great patriarchs of Judaism.

Originally conceived as a system of religious interpretation, the Gematria was only used to intrepret the symbols in Hebrew, Aramaic, and Greek texts, but it was applied to Latin texts of the seventeenth century as well. The widely held belief in the divine right of kings made the Gematria a system of astrology applied in the core to Cabalistic diagrams made for the names, titles, and events in a king's life. These were cast, and the diagram was used to prove divine guidance in the king's life.

In modern times, the Cabalist system has been combined with the Pythagorean theory of numbers to result in the science of Numerology. Practitioners believe that all numbers are in rhythm with the universe, and that letters in the alphabet are related to numbers, and every condition has its own peculiar vibration. This belief may be the source of the modern concept of "good vibrations."

Some believe that if you adopt a name with a numerological value with the right vibrations you will make your fortune. Numerologists hold the key to which names match up with which professions.

The Gematria, in combination with Pythagoras contributed to the invention of the alphabet. The use of letters to make words superseded hieroglyphics in Asia Minor between 1500 and 1000 B.C. There were no separate symbols for numbers; alphabet characters represented specific numbers, so there could be both an obvious and a hidden meaning in any given passages of words.

There was no official grammar, and each writer developed his own. Left-to-right writing was the norm, while Hebrew and Arabic were scripted right-to-left. Letters were sometimes interchangeable, as it was possible for words to have different spellings and more than one meaning and numerical value. The letter *jod*, for example, may mean one or ten, and the letter *shin* may mean three or three hundred.

Hebrew letters were not only designs but had secondary symbolism. Thus *vau*, the letter for six, was also a nail and, in another meaning, signified the womb.

The Tetragrammaton, which is YHVH in Hebrew, or 10-5-6-5, adds up to 26, the sacred number of Yahweh. The letter for Yahweh (*JHU*) in the Pythagorian triangle is 543 – this is the number of Moses and stands for one of the titles of God.

The Pythagorian triangle was also known as the Eye of Horus. Symbolizing the sun, the Egyptians called the three arms of the triangle Isis, Osiris, and Horus, and the three letters IOH are IVH, which the Egyptians applied to the triangle, were a secret formula which held the key to the Universe.

One interpretation says that 543 symbolized the three components of all existence which was three, representing spirit; four, representing matter; and five, representing spirit and matter in material form.

According to the Cabala, the manifestations of God are divided into three phases which form the basis of the three triads of Sepheroti in the Cabalistic Tree of Life.

Matter can be divided into gases, liquids, and solids, and the essence of existence can be derived from the three elements: air, fire, and water.

According to the Cabala, God and Satan have the same number: 364. On the three-hundred-sixty-fifth day of the year, which is sometimes termed the Day of Atonement, Satan can't accuse people.

Sir Isaac Newton, Bacon, and Spinoza are just three of the many fine minds who have been interested in the Cabala and found merit in studying the numbers.

The Cabala has attracted mathematicians who have made brilliant discoveries related to numbers. John Parker discovered that there is a perfect relationship between the circumference of a circle and its diameter. These congruencies have led to the thought that conclusive proof may be found in the Bible of a system of letters and their symbolistic meaning.

One example of Cabalism at work (and one that demonstrates its complexities) is the outcome when the letter Jod or ten is taken as the radius of a circle. The circumference will equal (almost) the measure of the perimeter of a square which measures 16 units on each side. The sixteen in the Cabalistic sense is 5 + 6 + 5, which is the equivalent of HVH or Eve. So this symbolic number can be seen to represent Eve in the Bible.

CANDLES

Light repels darkness, and God made light first. Light averts evil and melancholy. Candles are part of worship in many religions. On the altar they signify God's presence. Candlemas, which celebrates Jesus speaking at the temple, takes place forty days after the birth of Christ on Christmas.

Candles appear in Macbeth, and in the sixteenth century an unlit candle was sometimes carved on gravestones to symbolize the shortness of life and the mastery of death.

The Romans represented Vesta, goddess of the hearth, as well as Venus, goddess of love, with candles. The Hebrew menorah bears nine candles and signifies God's protection. It also symbolizes the nine lamps of Heaven (the planets). The seven-branched Babylonian candlestick represented the tree of life and was a precursor to our modern Christmas tree.

CIRCLE
The circle has always been symbol of the sacred. It represents totality and, therefore, God.

When Christian missionaries asked Native Americans to represent their god, the Indians sometimes drew a circle with feathers coming from it. Red feathers pointed in and black out, representing the way power moves – inward and outward.

The circle stands for eternity and spacelessness as there is no above and below. Like the wheel, it represents cyclical movement.

The circle is a prehistoric symbol and appears on early artifacts and drawings. It can be seen on mandalas, used as an aid to concentration and visualization, which combines the circle, the square (a cross), and the lotus or flame. The word *mandala* derives from the Arabic *al mandal*, which means circle. Tibetans try to make the self the center of the mandala, thus entering Buddhahood.

Romulus, who built Rome, put at its center an altar surrounded by a circular rampart. Towns have centers, around which local activity revolves. When pitching tents for the night, Native Americans put them in a circle.

The circle represents movement as opposed to the static square.

COLOR
Color is a feminine concept. The spiritual human is attracted to color. Form and color are male/female concepts. Form is the realist, the tangible, the male, and can be ugly or beautiful. Color is the fleeting female, encircling and poetic. Color

stirs the emotions. Color and love go together. Color has always been an important component of religious worship. Information about the symbolic value of individual colors can be found in this book listed under each color's name.

CONSONANTS

The three most important consonants (for our purposes) are B, which is the builder; L, or indirect activity; and D, which solidifies order.

The number associated with B is two, and its color is indigo. Bs have the ability to construct and apply in the material and spiritual world. B is both materialistic and spiritual. B is the builder, the female spirit, the people-pleaser, and unfolds by education. B lacks initiative, and is noted for duality. These people make excellent arbitrators for those who desire peace and, because of their duality, see problems from both sides. The bad B is a destroyer and a liar.

B is the first consonant. The Hebrew *b* stands for *beth*, which means house. It shows strength in applying lessons learned. B puts plans to work. Order and perfection are aspects of the letter. Mother – spirit and the domestic life – resonate in B. B is the symbol of power to open, whether it's one's mouth to speak or to read in literature. Beth, the house, is one of prayer. The Hebrews and the Africans both made piles of stones in which their deity dwelt. These edifices eventually evolved into our Western churches of today.

The letter C indicates the power of maleness. C presents the power of creativity in all undertakings. It signifies man as the thinker. It's a "controlling" letter. C, for example, creates through the brain, the mouth, and the sex organs. C is a restless letter and is impatient with other psyches not as quick as its own.

In Hebrew, D is symbolized by a door that is ajar. It means hard work. People of the D are not gamblers but behave straightforwardly. D people like to work, but if they happen to be a negative D, they are masters of self-pity, and they are susceptible to diseases of the abdomen and larynx. D people love home and country and are patriotic but do not become inspired by things. They establish ideas and will always be forthright.

The number associated with D is four and its color is dark blue. D shows strength of character, firmness, and is honest. D is a fair businessman but has set opinions. He loves his work. D is generous to others. Ds are close to nature. The lower Ds are stubborn – they won't give in during an argument.

G in the old days was symbolized by a camel on his knees, waiting for his burden. Today, G symbolizes kindness, strength, endurance, and truth – to name but a few qualities.

An H person can foretell the future and loves being at home. A touch Taurean in his tastes, H could be a psychic.

L's number is 30 and its color is purple. Ls are instigators and are background people. Ls go to the root of the matter; they are prone to great inertia and are lazy. An L makes a good boss who signs papers and oversees the work of others. The letter L is a form of the oxbow. It has two qualities. When it is capital, L lashes out and goads on. As a small l its inertia takes over. Ls make good leaders and have a good memory for facts that are ordered.

The number of M is 40 and its color is light blue. Ms are intellectual, with positive opinions and a great will. Ms either live the life of a happy socialite or a depressed human being. As a socialite, the M will do everything to get someone else to take his responsibility. As a depressed person, the M takes on all burdens. Ms are everyday people (not leaders) and are typical Taureans. They have good senses of humor.

CORNUCOPIA

Also known as the "horn of plenty," the cornucopia comes to us through the legend of Zeus, who overcame his father Kronos, and whose mother, Earth, gave the horn of plenty to

humans as a gift of appreciation. The horn eventually became the property of the river god, Akeloos, and symbolized the riches brought by rivers – crops, prosperity, and commerce. The horn of plenty symbol appeared often in Renaissance paintings. America, with its untouched riches, became represented by the cornucopia. The horn of plenty can be found in the Great Seals of Idaho and Wisconsin.

The Danes always end their banquets with a cornucopia on the table flowing with chocolates and other delicacies. The Latin American piñata comes from the tradition of the horn of plenty.

CREATION

In Egypt there are two themes of the world's creation: 1) that it was the work of Ptah, the Great Artificer, and 2) that the world was brought to life by the word of Thaut, who spoke and brought it into existence.

Osiris was also known as Unnefer, the Solar Fire. His name means the "many-eyed." In Greece, Iris was the rainbow and messenger to Juno and the rest of the gods.

Ptah has his symbol in art – the Scarabaeus or Scarab beetle.

In Mexico, a beetle symbolized the letter L and that meant the power of God.

Among the Celts, the beetle was called Haul, the word for sun. From Haul we get the English word holy. The German word for holy is heil and its god is Ella – which means the god that has existed forever.

The God Pan is Greek, but, surprise, in another incarnation he's also Egyptian. In Egyptian lore he belonged to a group of eight gods. And Pan is reproduced in Egyptian art exactly as he is in Greek Art – with the face and legs of a goat.

In Latin, *pan* means universal, and Pan is the root of the word *panacea*.

Another version of Pan was a Japanese diety. The national cheer *Banzai* means "the light of the great fire of life." In modern Japan, *Nippon* means "Fountain or source of light." Pan is the godfather of Spain, and is the root of the word for French bread – *pain*. The Pansy is also named after him. In the southern United States, there is a pansy that blooms all winter in the snow – surely the hardiest of blooms.

In Egypt, Pan was also known as Min, and the chief town of his worship was Kptos.

CRESCENT MOON

The lovely crescent moon is a symbol of many gods and goddesses, but it is especially sacred to Hecate, the patron goddess of Byzantium. She appeared on the coat of arms of that city in ancient times. Another goddess of the moon was Diana (Artemis), who had a famous temple at Ephesus in Asia Minor. Moon goddesses had their day in ancient times, but with the advent of Christianity, they have died out. St. Paul fought powerfully against the worship of Diana, and eventually Christianity blotted out her worship, replacing her with the Virgin Mary, also represented with the crescent moon. In 1698, in Vienna, the symbol of the crescent was removed from the Church of St. Stephen, thus ending the association of the crescent with the Virgin Mary.

In 1453, the Turks captured Constantinople from the Roman Empire and rode through the city bearing the crescent moon on their banners. Thus, the crescent became associated with the Turks. From the Turks, the symbol moved to other Arab countries, and became the universal symbol of Islam.

Today, the use of this symbol seems to be waning, as Libya and Egypt removed the crescent from their flags in recent years. Six other countries, however, still use it.

CROSS

A symbol of Christianity, the cross had symbolic
meaning before it assumed its religious connotation.
It has been found in China and Africa. It appears on
Bronze Age stones in Scandinavia. It was regarded as a magical symbol. It brought good luck and diverted evil. (Think of
its use in staving off vampires.) It is thought, in some quarters,
that the Cross, found in rock carvings, is a solar symbol. Others say it's the symbol of earth. Its points represent the four
directions: North, south, east, and west. Assyrian belief says it's
the symbol of universal gods. People wore cross charms to
keep away evil in ancient times.

After Christ was crucified, Christians didn't use the sign
of the cross as their religious symbol for several hundred years.
It was connected with executioners. Christians used the cross,
finally, about 200 A.D. in the catacombs. In 312 A.D., Constantine had a dream in which a cross, denoted as a Christian
symbol, meant he would prevail in war. Constantine won a
battle, and the cross was then carried on banners by the
Roman Army. Constantine introduced religious freedom in the
Roman Empire during the next year. After the cross was out-
lawed as a means of execution, it became fully embraced by
the Christians as their symbol of Christ. It stood for his death
and suffering. And, most important, it symbolized the Resurrection, becoming a symbol of faith to Christians everywhere.

D

DEER

The symbol for St. Kentigern is a stag.

Antelopes are inscribed on the coat of arms of the Duke of Abercorn.

During a fierce encounter between Siva and his father-in-law Daksha, both gods and mortals fled. The Deer leaped into the sky, where it may be seen in the constellation we call Orion, pursued by the great hunter, Siva.

DOG

The Egyptians sometimes mummified dogs, which resembled jackals. In Persia, the dog was identified with Ormuz, and the Parsees to this day revere them. Sirius, the Dog Star, is part of a constellation called the Great Dog.

In India, the dog Saramas is a symbol of dawn. The ancient Indian tale of dawn goes this way: Rays of sun or rain clouds are stolen by the powers of the darkness of night and are hidden in the night sky. Then Dawn appears and runs across the dark sky like a dog following a scent. After Dawn comes Indra, the God of Light ready to battle the powers of darkness. Saramas, the dawn dog, is supposed to be a greyhound. This dog was referred to by Dante.

The dog is also the symbol of guardianship. In India he watches the door of heaven during the night and barks as morning appears.

DOLPHIN

The Greeks believed the dolphin to be friendly and intelligent, just as modern science has confirmed. The dolphin is a symbol of joy and freedom. It is a friend to sea voyagers and has been said to rescue many in times of trouble. Dolphins were the

friends of Neptune. The Greeks thought of dolphins as saviors of the shipwrecked, and representations of dolphins could often be found on the coins of ancient seaside towns.

DOORWAY

Entering a house, one passes through its doorway and enters a world of the unknown; almost anything may occur. This symbolic movement is also found in entering a forest, passing through a wall, or going through Alice's looking glass. The door represents the passage of one state to another – to a new life. The door itself opens to opportunity.

It is a meeting place between material and supernatural conditions, and it's bad luck to step on the threshold. That's why brides are carried by their husbands across the threshold of the couple's new home. In the world of superstition, a piece of iron placed in the doorway keeps away evil spirits, which have an aversion to iron. This superstition accounts for horseshoes being a good-luck symbol.

Doorways of treasure rooms were always guarded by malevolent creatures to frighten robbers away. (Spiritually, these creatures also represented the difficulty the hero would face in gaining entrance.) The monsters scared away the unworthy who were too timid to fight dragons to gain treasure – spiritual or real.

DRAGON

One of the most ancient symbols is the dragon. Dragons are found in stories from all the cultures of humankind, and they are not always evil. The Chinese, of course, decorate with the dragon, as do the Norse and the Irish.

In early times, the drawn Chinese dragon figure was rather two-dimensional, with the object simply representing a

god. With the development of civilization, the depiction of
dragon became three-dimensional and more shapely. By the
Shang dynasty, the dragon was designed as an imperial symbol. Dragon carvings were often used for religious purposes in
concert with other animal forms.

The dragon can symbolize either good or evil, and,
besides being the evil snake in the Garden of Eden, it is also
a deliverer from poisonous snakes.

The dragon is described by all as a spirit of fire and water
that lives in the ocean or flies through the heavens. Blood
from the heart of a dragon gave the slayer wisdom. And it
could be a guardian – sometimes of treasure, sometimes of a
princess, or even of the golden fleece.

Many heroes of legend did battle with dragons. Dragons
were part of the world of both gods and man. They could
make eclipses occur by swallowing the sun and capture rain
clouds. Man might fall through a dragon's temptation. The
dragon was part of the mysteries of ancient secret thought.
The Chinese painted it and believed it to be related to the
mystic pearl. The dragon encircles the North Pole in the heavens. Once it contained the Pole Star itself.

Among the symbols of the ancients was the constellation
Draco. Draco is the guardian of the pole because it marked the
limit of stars in the ancient world. It is the pathway for the
sun, the moon, and the planets. This Draco is at the heart of
the fixed stars which appear to be guarded by it.

The zodiac is the oldest artifact of ancient thought that
we have. While the zodiac isn't well understood in this age, it
still survives. As a symbol, we hold on to it for dear life. The
dragon is a creation of the spirit of mankind. The zodiac
guards the pathway to the heavens and the way into those
realms.

The Earth, the sun, and the moon have a relationship to
the lore of the astrologer. As the moon affects the ocean, the
sun and moon together affect the Earth. The meeting of the
sun and moon in an eclipse is at the head and tail of the

dragon. This is not understood by modern astrologers. But the old astrologers realized its importance.

To understand the planets (and especially the fixed stars) is to realize they travel and circle around Draco. Draco oversaw the changing stars and is related to the earth because of the pull of the sun and the moon. The Golden Dragon, or Draco, is in the midst of the zodiac and, to the Chaldean astronomers, it was the central symbol of the whole sky. Draco hangs above the serpent stars that lie at the horizon – Hydra and Serpens.

The dragon is dark and bright – springing from the earth and heavens. The dragon is placed over the universe like royalty over its subjects. Such as it is, the dragon is the master symbol to ancient astrologers. It is a sign not in the zodiac but of great importance to it. It is the thirteenth sign. By its placement in the heavens, one can judge the seasons of the year. Mercury is the planet most closely associated with the Dragon.

The dragon is the greatest symbol of time – the past. Draco was watched on Easter as Christians awaited the coming of Christ. Its coils lay about the heavens due north and hung at its zenith at the south of the pole star. Altar and Regulas are in the east and west of Draco, and form the arms of the cross in the Easter skies.

The conqueror Cadmus was warned by Zeus to remember the Dragon of the North when worshipping Zeus.

The dragon is to China what the eagle is to America. Some people think the Western mind has trouble discerning all the subtle meanings of the Chinese dragon. The Chinese dragon symbolizes royalty and power, clouds, rain, and floods. Water is a source of good as well as evil, and the Chinese dragon rules the rain-giving gods of the water. He is also the spirit of change. He has the power of invisibility and can transform himself. When he breathes, his breath becomes clouds on which he rides. He goes to the sky at the time of the spring equinox. At the autumn equinox, he plunges into the depths of the ocean. He sleeps in the winter, and awakens again in the spring.

The dragon is said to eat the sun during an eclipse.

The dragon is the God of Thunder and shows himself in the rice paddies as rain or as dark clouds. As the royal dragon ascends, he belches forth a ball. That ball is thunder. The ball in the dragon's mouth is also a pearl, believed to be the concrete spirit of the moon taken from the secret workings of nature, which is represented by the oyster shell which forms the pearl. Thus we have a charm against fire.

There are four dragons in China: The Celestial Dragon, which upholds the heavens; the Spiritual Dragon of wind and rain; the Earth Dragon of rivers and streams; and the Dragon of Hidden Treasure, who watches over the treasure concealed from men.

Each dragon has its own color. The blue dragon is the most revered of the four because blue is the color of the east. The blue dragon symbolizes water and its spirit. The yellow dragon is the divine manifesting power.

As far back as 2200 B.C., Yan, the Dragon, was one of six symbolic figures painted on the emperor's upper garment.

The combination of the Dragon, Lion, and Eagle produce the Gryphon, which has an eagle's head, a lion's body with wings, and a serpent's tail.

E

EAGLE

The eagle is the symbol of God. As the United States' emblem, it is omnipotent. One early version of the Eagle symbol has the letter S in its forehead, designating Spiritus, and the Star-Cross of the God of Light.

EARLY BELIEFS

Ancient peoples thought that our souls were composed of four elements – fire, air, water, and earth. When united, the elements formed fire and became a flame. It was believed that, after death, the soul was immersed in water and its impurities were washed away. It was then refined by fire. The supreme spirit was imagined to be a flame of fire which burned into infinity.

The Chinese believed that the supreme being of fire was a fixed point for the souls which had been cleansed, and they circled about the Supreme One. Sun rays symbolized the eternal spirit.

One symbol had the letters *IHS* which meant that Jesus Christ was identified with the eternal flame. The sun symbolized the primal source which brought together the light and warmth of creation. The S of Spiritus appears on a sun sign as well as the crescent moon.

Another combination of letters from antiquity that symbolize Christ is *YHS*, which stand for Yeshua – another name for Jesus. The *Y* itself is a symbol from truly ancient times, and its shape is a source of reverence for the Chinese.

The Sun, an ancient symbol of God, was sometimes represented as a wheel. The rays were spokes, and the Supreme Being was regarded as the center.

The letter *S* sometimes shows up in the ancient symbology. Like the *Y*, it stands for a supreme being, in this case Brahma (the breath of all creation), who was also known as Lord of the Stars.

Brahma was considered to be like a spider – the spinner of creation – but he's also the sun.

The Egyptians defined spirit as fire, and a similar belief may be found among the Hindus.

Belief in the oversoul is a feature of some classic literature. We are all parts of the whole, and God is our oversoul, or the soul in all of nature. In this concept, man is a spark. The oversoul was sometimes called the cloud of the unknown.

Fire symbolizing God appeared to Moses as the burning bush in the Bible. God identified Himself from the flames as *I Am* and spoke to Moses about His people being enslaved to the Egyptians.

One sun symbol is decorated with the number 33, a number revered in Egypt.

EGG

The mystery of life lies in the egg, so it is a symbol of rebirth. According to the beliefs of many early civilizations, the world was egg-shaped. The myths of the Chinese, Hindus, and ancient Egyptians are based on the concept of an egg-shaped universe. They believe the world was hatched from an egg which came from God.

The Egyptians thought the god who laid the egg of the universe was Ra, the god of eternal life. He was thought to have been born from an egg, too, and is often depicted breaking out of a shell.

One Greek myth has it that the Great Goddess and the snake Phion hatched the egg of the universe and produced the Greek god Apollo. Snake eggs generally hatch in the sun, and Apollo is associated with the sun.

Alchemy, which had its origins in Egypt and was thought to be occult and representative of the hidden life, grew out of the mystery promulgated by the egg. In alchemy, blood, sperm, and water were believed to be the foundations of life.

The cock was the Greek bird associated with resurrection (the sun rising daily brought forth the cock) and was sacred to

the son of Apollo, Aesculapius, a famous physician who was
thought to be able to bring the dead back to life.

ELEMENTS

Early man believed the four elements – fire, water, earth, and air –
were a manifestation of divine
power. The soul was thought to be
made up of all four elements which
when taken together took the form
of fire.

The Chinese Taoists, however,
believed there were five elements:
water, wood, fire, earth, and metal.
The belief was that they conquered each other according to
divine law. Thus wood conquered earth; earth conquered
water; water conquered fire; fire conquered metal; and metal
conquered wood.

The Chinese Buddhists later accepted the Greek and
Indian idea of four elements and one more – ether – to make
five.

The symbolism of the elements made earth a square,
water a circle, fire a triangle, air a crescent, and ether a jewel
– the jewel in the lotus – which topped off the diagram of the
conquered elements.

A diagram symbolizing the elements may be found in
Buddhist monasteries in Japan and Tibet, and throughout Asia
wherever the Chinese have roamed.

Triangular temples supported by five elements symbolized
that gods were worshipped in the temple and presided over
the four elements that represent creation and the natural
world.

Venus was the Queen of Heaven, Earth, and Hell – and
the four elements were among her attributes; the numbers
associated with her were three, four, and seven.

THE EYE AND THE LIGHT

The Eye of Shiva, the Eye of Horus, and the eye of Zeus were all symbols for the Divine presence everywhere. Wotan of Norse mythology was also portrayed as one-eyed and as a symbol of the Sun.

St. Matthew believed that one eye symbolized light, that the light of the soul is in the eye.

The two circles eventually meet as one and represent light. God is often symbolized by a circle and, in ancient Mexico, the God was represented as a circle – as was Granez of Persian mythology and Assur of the Assyrians.

The Egyptians portrayed God as the eye of the universe. A dot in the circle meant that the deity (the dot) was surrounded by eternity. The Egyptian eye, or udjat, was used as an amulet to keep evil away. It promoted well-being. It was painted on coffins and was worn by soldiers in battle. The Assyrian sun god was Sin, which translates to sun in English, and meant the light of the sun.

The representation of the Chaldean deity, Eusoph, was the Light of Life and a triangle. The Hindu Aum is similarly symbolized. The Egyptian triangle represented Nature.

Over the Delphic oracle the letter E was inscribed. Because the letter has five points it was considered to be a five. But some mystics believed that it meant Thou Art, which translated to Jehovah – the living God. The five points of the E were equivalent to the five points of Solomon's Seal. E is the letter of light and is sometimes portrayed as the Eye of Light.

The letter T was also a symbol of Light. T was the tau cross and, according to Ezekiel, was the letter branded in the forehead of the elect.

The Mayan T was the same letter as the Latin T, and it was also expressed as an equilateral triangle. The Greek D (delta) is shaped like a triangle, and the meaning of D and T is the same.

The *viva* or *vivas* spoken in Latin countries is related to Vivasvat, a sanskrit name for the sun.

The study of language touches the very soul of man and opens his heart and philosophy to understanding.

The ancient Mexicans were named CoxCox or the Great Great Light. The Teutons claim descent from Tuisco – the Aryan god of light.

The name *Jesse* means ever-existing great light. In Cornwall, the name Jozon means sunlight, and this name underlies such surnames as Jones and Johns.

Santa Claus translates into the "Light of the Great Orb of God." The ancients believed that anything round was a symbol of the Orb of Being.

The symbol Op, meaning eye, occurs frequently in Europe, the word itself containing the letters *op. Europe* is a symbol of the splendor of morning. Ethiopia contains *op* as well.

F

FESTIVALS

The Druids passed stories from one generation to the next by word of mouth. Knowledge was not written down. Writing was unknown until well past the introduction of the Bards. The family records of the Bard's patrons were handed down through stories and songs.

The Druids also inculcated superstition in the minds of the people, as did the Brahmins of India.

In India two festivals are celebrated: Holi comes toward the end of March, and Divali is in the fall. Holi is a bad woman, and a house is built in which her effigy is placed. The house is then set on fire. Divali is a housecleaning festival. It is dedicated to the goddess Kali, who likes sulfur. Sulfur is added to the bonfires that are made in celebration of Divali, and this pleases Kali. The fire also destroys the malaria that is present in the autumn.

Holi is a festival of the poor classes, and Divali is celebrated by all classes. Divali means the festival of lamps. All buildings are whitewashed for the festival. The lamps that are lit attract the malaria mosquitoes, which are destroyed by the bonfires. The goddess of cholera, smallpox, and snakes joins in the celebration.

In Scotland, Halloween is the occasion for the Procession of Lamps, which the Scots make of turnips, carved with the faces of the sun and the moon. The origins of this procession are lost in the annals of time, but since it takes place in the fall, it may be an offshoot of Divali.

FIRE WORSHIP

In Brittany, there is fire worship in an elaborate ceremony that is thought to be exactly like certain prehistoric ceremonies. Apparently, fire worship has to do with the growth of crops as the hymns sung are about the fire as it relates to crops. *An Tan* is the shout that goes up when worshipping fire. Mothers shove their children before the flames and call on Saint Peter to bless them.

In Greece, women jumped through flames crying, "I leave my sins behind me."

In the Hindu religion, fire was made by twisting crossed sticks, and was used for the sacred fire in the Hindu temples.

On St. Vitus Day, June 15, a cart wheel was set afire on the summit of a mountain, and the people worshipped the flaming wheel.

San Tan means holy fire in the Celtic language.

FISH

At a small church in Sussex, England, there is a fish design on the entrance tiles. There is a fish symbol in Scotland at Kincardineshire. In Peru, there is a temple from an unknown race dedicated to the fish god, Pachacamoc, who symbolizes the Creator.

Fish motifs appear in the Mayan ruins of Central America.

FLAGS

Flags are social symbols, not generally displayed to ornament the body. They serve as symbols of unity for the population. The Supreme Court has decided that burning the American flag is "free speech." The American Legion has undertaken to change the Constitution to protect the flag from burning because soldiers who serve this country use the flag as a symbolic rallying point, and are deeply disgusted to think their symbol can be burned with impunity. I hope the American Legion wins this change in the Constitution as the symbol of America needs this kind of protection.

The Tikopic people of the South Pacific use a piece of white barkcloth as their flag. They fly it to celebrate the end of the yam planting season. While visiting on another island, they set up this selfsame flag. The Tikopians' flag was fashioned after those they saw on European ships, and it served as a warning to keep the populace away from the newly planted yams.

In the Philippines, a bloodied flag was flown when a head was hung in a house after a battle. This symbolized a successful headhunt.

In Sioux country, the Indians displayed a flag of white cloth with a bundle of tobacco and corn, which meant to other Sioux who saw it that a peaceful meeting was going to take place nearby and that others should follow to partake of the feasting.

Modern flags were invented in the Orient, and they were brought to the Europeans by the Saracens. The Orientals used cloth flags at horse and bull races, and to designate the travel of princes. They were more than symbolic ostentation, however, and carried messages in their colors. Yellow was the color of the flag of the Emperor. Some Mongol cloth banners bore the likeness of a prince, and the term *banner* came to mean the social group related to it. The Manchus used the Mongol banner too – but only for military purposes.

Among the Philippines, at a later date, the flag came to symbolize marriage. A pole was set out in front of the house of the newlyweds. On the third day of the ceremonies it was taken down, then hoisted again for another three days.

During the Second World War this flag ceremony was altered and red flags were used – probably after the Japanese system. In Japan, flags were associated with holidays and marked boys' ceremonies as well as funerals and memorials for the dead. During World War Two, Japanese homeowners who had a son in the war would take a bamboo tree and cut off its leaves, leaving just the top ones. Then a national flag would be tied beneath the leaves and the tree would remain there till the son's return from war.

As signals, flags convey information as well as ideas and emotions that can be quite complex. In the country, farmers sometimes hoist flags to attract the attention of the milkman – meaning they want milk. The only proscription for such a flag is that it not be made of red material. This is because a red flag means road work ahead. The color red is often used for flags that signify danger.

Complex flag signals are used at sea, and this flag language was especially sophisticated in the eighteenth century. Such signal flags are symbolic in color, shape, pattern, and position, and are employed to communicate an internationally understood code.

Some simple flags have specific meanings. A yellow flag with a Q in the center means quarantine or an infectious disease aboard ship. A white flag always means surrender.

A yellow flag with a black ball stands for the letter I. A flag with alternating yellow and blue stripes symbolizes the letter G. Both of these flags are rectangular, but others are pennant-shaped. An alphabetically arranged message can be very cumbersome – so some flags mean more than just individual letters. If you put together the yellow flag with a black ball in the center, and a blue cross on a white background (the letter X), the combination IX means "I have received serious damage in a collision." There are said to be seventy-eight thousand combinations in all.

This signal flag code can also be used with the morse code for flags and semaphore signaling.

Semaphore is a visual code – not the color, but the relative position of the flag to the body of the flagman indicates the meaning. The flags are used individually or in conjunction with others, which gives the key to the meaning.

In using flag morse code, the meaning is not in the position but in the sequence. This is a flow of sequences and short pulses to carry the message. The flags are waved rapidly or in a short or long arc, giving different meanings.

To make a salute, a flag is dipped slowly then raised quickly. A flag at half-mast always means mourning. A flag flown upside down is a signal of distress.

Some flag flying is even more symbolic – representing ideas or objects of value. The white flag of surrender means a plea to stop fighting, and the relinquishment of the ship to the winner. The black flag was piratical and stood for a whole attitude toward law and order, as well as property and sovereignty. A red flag is often used to indicate revolution.

FLEUR-DE-LIS

The fleur-de-lis is a symbol of life. In design it resembles a plant, but it's unclear whether that plant was meant to be a lily or an iris. (*Fleur-de-lis* means lily in French.) The fleur-de-lis appeared in Egyptian and Mesopotamian works of art and was seen in Europe during the Middle Ages.

The fleur-de-lis was thought to represent Christ as the Light of the World. The "flower of light" is seen with a halo – with flames issuing therefrom.

The symbol spread throughout Europe and can be found in hundreds of coats of arms. In France, the fleur-de-lis was seized from the monarchy during the revolution. The fleur-de-lis remained in use in other parts of Europe, however, and today the symbol has returned to France under the aegis of the fashion industry. In America, the symbol is used by the Boy Scouts.

FLOWERS AND GARDENS

Primitive man thought that islands were sacred gardens and a place where souls gathered. The Greeks called the Scilly Islands the Hesperides, and were fond of naming islands Fortune or Blessed. Scilly means innocence and blessed.

In England, Avesbury is modeled after the Egyptian Temple Gardens, a manmade garden with pools and springs and hills.

The rose was identified with Christ and, before Christianity, with the Virgin Sophia. The Bride in the Rose of Sharon is another icon. In the story *Romance of the Rose*, a rose turns into a maiden. The Persian Eden was known as Yima's Garden – a walled garden.

In Spencer's *Fairie Queen*, the rose is a symbol of God's heavenly grace. The Orchard of the Rose (the Garden of Grace) is filled with strange plants and the roses were flowers of flame and stars.

Among firelike flowers are azaleas, peonies, and hollyhocks.

The star-flowered jasmine was the symbol for the Bright and Morning Star sprung from the root of Jesse. Jasmine was sacred in Ceylon. The Ceylonese pyramid, the Dagaba, was covered with jasmine blooms and on occasion buried in flowers.

In Celtic, the word *rose* means dew, and the Orchard of the Rose is identified thus with the new Jerusalem.

A golden iris marks the arms of Florence, Italy, a city which came from the bosom of Fiesole. The word *flower* means Living Lord of Life and Living God of Light. *Fiesole* means soul's fire.

A carnation is the flower of the cross and symbolized the supreme spirit.

The thistle is a holy plant. In Anglo Saxon, *thistle* is the word for the Great Bear Constellation.

The Lady's Finger, or Lady's Slipper, is sacred to the Virgin Mary.

The Garden of King Solomon's Bride is described as bearing pomegranates in an orchard and symbolized fertility. The pomegranate is a symbol of the Virgin Mary as well.

FOUR

The ancient Greeks divided the world and the universe into four parts; four became their universal number. It stood for order and against chaos. There are four seasons and four parts to human life: childhood, youth, maturity, and age. There are air, water, earth, and fire. There are four virtues: prudence, temperance, justice, and fortitude.

There is a symbol "four" that represents fire, and tetrakis stood among the Pythagoreans for God. In Mexico, four was represented as *Can* and meant Heaven (perhaps Cancun is named for this ancient deity). Can was then subject to the Creator, and was entrusted with watching the pillar that holds up the sky.

There are four gospels and four winds of the earth. Comfort seems to exist in the number four – and it symbolizes much.

FOX

The fox usually symbolizes cunning and slyness. In the Medieval days the fox was characterized as the Devil and, along with the cat and the rabbit, was often associated with witchcraft.

In the Medieval literature of France and Germany, the fox was known as Reynard and was used to satirize the current events of the times. Reynard shows up in the classic French version of "The Fox and the Crow." A *corbeau* had cheese in his beak that Reynard wanted. The fox flattered the crow into thinking that he could sing with a most beautiful voice and, when the crow parted his beak to sing, the cheese fell out and into the mouth of Reynard.

Some of Chaucer's tales speak of Reynard the fox as early as 1481. In the Chaucerian stories, the fox always had grandiose ideas, but his schemes never bore fruit. The fox was supposed to have a magic ring with a three-colored stone. The green was for invisibility, the red stone turned night into day, and the white cured all illnesses. In another story, the cunning and sly Reynard promised his Queen a crystal ball with which she could observe events anywhere she wished. But the promised globe never showed up, as it existed only in Reynard's imagination.

G

GEMINI

The ancients regarded the symbol for Gemini as a symbol for the Supreme Being. In Scotland, a two-circle ornament was found and believed to symbolize the Duality of God. On one monument in Scotland, the circles are shown as a wheel and symbolize the solar chariot. This  same symbol was found etched on a gem that belonged to the Gnostics.

Poets wrote of Zeus that he took the form of a swan and loved a human named Leda. She gave birth to an egg out of which hatched the swans Castor and Pollux. The Greeks knew them as the Dioscuri, and they were usually seen riding white horses. White lambs were the usual offering to the Dioscuri who were not only representations of twin circles but of cherubs. These were featured on ornaments of the Renaissance. On one ornament there is a picture of the twins on either side of a vase. They appear as twin goats with Pan.

In Egypt, twins were symbolized by two lions, one of which was day and the other was night. Osiris was called the Lord of the Double Lions and the sun was called the Lion of the Double Lions.

The twin letter M means Light of the One in the Dorian alphabet. Twin peaks are also AA, like two breasts. In the Vedas, one of the As is white and the other black – they are twin sisters. The Chaldean God of Life was sometimes represented as AA or Aos. *Aos* means dawn in Greek and in Sanskrit – life. This Chaldean Aos symbolized Light, Spirit, and the Essence of the Great A.

GNOSTICS

The Gnostics conformed to the outside world and yet maintained their secret ideas and ways without letting outsiders know. Their basic tenet was to learn all they could but to let no one know them.

The Gnostics identified the Greek Hermes as well as the Egyptian Osiris with Christ, the Guider of Souls, and a jackal-headed figure symbolized Him as He was on the cross.

GOD SYMBOLS

Symbolic language is the tongue of faith. There is no way to speak of God but in symbols. Faith doesn't speak of an object and therefore can't be analyzed like an object.

The symbols of God taken from nature are found in the Bible. They come from the earth, on which man moves. God is represented by a rock. The word is an image of strength. It's not an adequate definition of God, but just one aspect.

The word *love* – from man's world – is also used to symbolize God. The Bible says "God is Love."

God spoken of through souls goes back to the New Testament. Jesus speaks of God as the Father. He is secret – there is no theoretical teaching about Him. St. John's speeches regarding God are all symbolic. Think of the parables.

The concept of God and the image of God are separate subjects for study. Built on a philosophical grounding, they've had a part of enormous importance to play in theology.

There is an unwritten law in the Bible of never representing God as an object among those He created. He is above all. There are just no representations of God. The fire in the burning bush, the fire on Mt. Sinai when Moses was there, and the voice of God to Elijah which was a still, small voice are as close to representation as we get.

Isaiah saw God in a vision sitting on a throne. And in the New Testament the Spirit is seen as a dove. The Book of Revelation also contains a vision of the throne of God. While the Bible prohibits direct images of God, the Christian Church doesn't. In the Middle Ages, the Trinity was religiously depicted in painting, and the Throne of God has an old man on it. It's said that the Church didn't follow the Bible ordinance and depicted God as a recognizable image. God is also depicted as the all-seeing eye in a triangle – such as we have on our money. Pictures of Christ are usually sentimentalized and are thus of small importance.

The symbols of God taken from nature are frequent in the Old Testament. He is the "Book of my Salvation" and people are taken beneath God's wings.

Fountains and wells and springs are also used to symbolize God. These waters are meant to satiate thirst when people drink from them. God's fountain is a fountain of life as well as the fountain of salvation. God, from Heaven, is depicted as light. God wears a garment of light. When He wears it, the garment is contrasted with darkness which folds before the light that is shed before Him.

Heaven is where God lives, and his throne is there. *Heaven* is sometimes used synonymously with *God*. Jesus asks: "The Baptism of John, whence was it – from Heaven or from man?" (Matthew 21:25)

There is no limiting God to just Heaven. He may appear in Hell as well.

There are symbols linked to human life that pertain to the Bible. With the human body, the face is a symbol of light, as in "the Lord made His face to shine." He also turns his face away and casts men away from Him.

The symbols of arms and hands are symbols of the strength of God. They're mentioned in connection to victory in war.

The symbols eye and ear are symbolized into *behold* and *to hear*. *Mouth* is rarely used, but *the word of God* and *to speak* are commonly used throughout the Bible. The word *Lord* was used to symbolize Jesus beyond the meaning of Messiah. It's a word that Jews and non-Jews alike may use similarly.

King is also used to symbolize God. In the New Testament the king is a messianic Redeemer-King.

The symbolic word *shepherd* is used in the Old Testament regarding Christ. The word *Shepherd*, as it is used to describe Christ, is like *King* and *Lord* in power.

The word *Father* symbolizes different things in each testament. The Old Testament rarely uses it but it's commonly used in the New Testament. Indeed, it is the most-used name for God. He is the one above all others and is called *Father.*

Symbolic words such as *Savior, Judge,* and *Redeemer* are all parts of everyday life and refer back to it – law courts, judges, etc.

Eternity is, in the Old Testament, time without an ending. God is the Eternal King. In the New Testament, eternity means that God can't be measured by time. He's above the concept of time, the world, and its changes. There is no variableness of light and darkness.

God's holiness refers to His sinless state and the contrast between humans and God in this regard. Holiness is the divine background, not just a state of sinlessness.

God sits on His high throne. From the beginning, two qualities of the Christ have been shown: height and length of life. Height means God was superior to all people. He is high above us. It means what is sublime and worthy of adoration.

In language, height is more than God – height is equated with value. *Superior* is another word for God's high value. God the Most High simply means that He is superior to all beings.

Some believe that God lives in the sky. The sky itself is sometimes personified as a deity. Babylonians, Persians, and Grecians all believed that the sky god was a man who lived in the sky. The Babylonians called him Anu. He lived on his throne and stood every now and then.

Greeks called God Zeus. According to Greek belief, Zeus was the god in the sky. The Aryan Sky-God, *Siva,* and *Dyoum* shining, was originally applied to the sky.

In the Andaman Islands today, God is believed to be very old with a long white beard. He is thought to be shining brightly, like a fire. One group feels that God's face is covered and no one has seen it except for the Evil spirit, which saw his face once.

In Tierra del Fuego, the people believe that God can't be seen, but can be felt or heard. He is the wind and the sky – as big and as grand as the sky. Primitives all believed that God lives in the sky, as do many today.

Ancient Egyptians believed that the sky god was a woman and symbolized her as arching over her husband, the Earth. The sun, their child, rose and set out of her mouth.

The Stoics practiced religious beliefs that predated Christianity. They maintained that everything was God, and that we return to God through fire. Fire was God and made the world.

GOOSE

The goose was once a mystic bird. The goose also gave birth to the Egyptian god Ra. Images of geese were carved into the temple of the Gallic Mars, and geese carved in ivory were discovered at Lake Baikal.

The goose was a symbol of fertility to the Chinese, and also the Sumerians, who believed that the chariot of the god Gula was drawn by four white geese. To the men of ancient times the goose was a symbol of constancy and had immortality like the gods.

The Romans thought the goose to be a symbol of fate and vigilance, ever since a flight of geese had warned that the Gauls were attacking Rome.

St. Martin of Tours, who was a hermit, was once called to become a Bishop. The cackling of a goose disclosed his whereabouts to the elders, and he was forced to accept the office.

Since Queen Elizabeth, the royal table at Michaelmas has held a cooked goose. Don't forget the goose that laid the golden egg in folklore – it was a symbol of plenty.

The magic associated with these birds has disappeared; the goose now symbolizes a foolish person.

GREEN

The color green stands for nature and fertility. Because of the aridness of the desert, the Arabs use green in their flags. It also represents youth, rebirth and life in its infancy. In the sixteenth century, Protestants used the color in their symbols. It meant the new church – the break from the Catholic Church. Today, the color green stands for hope. It's associated with plants and pines which retain their color throughout the year. Philosophers who saw that evergreen plants don't die in winter associated them with life everlasting. Mistletoe bears these connotations, as does the Christmas tree.

The St. Andrew's cross of the Basque people is green. The design is British, but the colors are Cymric.

The color green also stands for freedom and was used as a symbol of liberty during the French Revolution. The Italian flag bears green in its insignia of freedom.

GREETING AND PARTING

There are a wide variety of greeting and parting symbols; the kiss, the formal handshake, the exchange of names and business cards. Our cultural greeting symbol is usually a smile or a wave of the hand.

H

Hammer
Hand
Heart
Heaven
Horse
Hosts of God
House

HAMMER

The hammer symbolizes work, the workweek and, most often, the smith. On the flag of Communist Russia, the hammer was combined with a symbol of industrial workmen, the sickle which symbolized farmwork.

The hammer has occult meanings too. Thor, the Norse god, could create lightning by throwing his hammer. And the people who remained Pagan in early times wore the hammer emblem to denote their belief in the old gods. The hammer became the symbol of "calling for order" in the halls of justice and at auctions. The English St. Eloi was a goldsmith and his hammer, as he was a saint, came to symbolize that profession.

God is supposed to be the Master Workman, working with his hammer and anvil. He is the architect of the universe.

HAND

The hand symbolizes power, mastery, and authority. The Roman Legions used the hand as an emblem. As a symbol of power, the hand represents God and all His aspects from love to punishment. The Arabs paint the Hand of Fatima on their doors as protection against evil. The open hand is a greeting: Peace all over the world. The clenched fist, used by the revolutionaries, represents the thrust of attack. The hand is a symbol of friendship, a consent, and a confirmation. The trade union banner of Europe displays a clasped hand as a symbol of solidarity and fraternity. The extended-hand symbol over the centuries came to mean the tenacity with which the mystics maintained their beliefs.

HEART

Plato said the soul resides in the heart, and that it oversees the emotions and intelligence. He also said that the most important organs in a human are his heart, genitals, and mind. He thought the heart, like the axis of a wheel, was the center of the human, and everything humans did depended on it.

The heart was venerated by the Hebrews and Christians, and is a symbol of love, courage, understanding, and devotion to them. To the alchemists, the heart was the symbol of the sun within the human being. Because love focuses on a specific center – the heart – in conjunction with the sun, the heart became a symbol of love.

The heart also stands for eternity. In a mummified body, it was the only organ left intact to ensure immortality.

In one edition of the Egyptian *Book of the Dead* there is an illustration of a man standing before balances, in which his heart is being weighed against a feather – as a test of his righteousness. Evil practitioners of sorcery would remove the heart and create evil with it.

The Christians adopted the heart symbol as their own, and it became associated with Jesus and the saints. The flaming heart is a symbol of religious fervor and, pierced by an arrow, means contrition and repentance.

HEAVEN
The Ladder of Perfection symbolizes the ascent of the soul. The Ladder of Virtues was a favored symbol of the roadway to God. One moved steadily on its rungs to perfection – a slow ascent as goodness increased. The goal of ascent is represented as fleur-de-Lis of light and as a star, or the Christ, as the "bright and morning star." Christ is the Pole Star and the only star to follow.

Christ was regarded as a stag as well as a star. He leapt from one virtue to the next. The stag is in the mountains. This is because the Psalmists and the mystics believed that they walked with the Lord – proceeding over the mountains of the heavenly landscape.

In allegory, mountains often represent meditation and heavenly communion. The legend of the Holy Grail emanates from this tradition and the grail was preserved at the summit of the Mountain of Salvation. This holy mountain was said to have three peaks made of gold, silver, and iron. The Hindus and Mongols, among others, said that the Mountain of Salvation was the home of the Trinity – Brahma, Vishnu, and Siva.

The star and the cross were symbols of the expected Messiah. The eagle was said to represent the promise of "they who wait on the Lord shall mount up with the wings of eagles."

The idea that the Spirit lives in a high place, was symbolized in the dove. Followers of God were said to be doves.

HORSE

On the island of Sein, in Brittany, there is an annual mistletoe ceremony that takes the residents all around their island, proceeded by musicians. Children lead a horse dressed in flowers, and this horse represented the Divine Mind of Reason.

Plato thought that the horse symbolized reason and opinion and, in a bad sense, confused fantasy.

Swedenborg says that the significance of the horse came from the ancient church, even in Greece. They placed the horse (four fiery horses) with the chariot of the sun, and thought of them as the god of wisdom and intelligence.

In speaking of the god of the Sea (Neptune), they also attributed horses to him.

With the birth of science, the Greek's story goes, came the intellectual principle. A flying horse symbolized them.

The Trojan horse was an intellectual ruse that used understanding to destroy walls.

The intellectual principle is symbolized by the Pegasus even today.

HOSTS OF GOD

The Moon symbolized the gatherer of the stars, and the stars were supposed to be the souls of the saints of Heaven, so the night sky with its stars was the Hosts of God made visible.

In most mythologies, night was the nursing mother of the stars, and was a beneficent being in itself.

The Moon was in charge of the stars, and the Lord of Hosts was the seven-fold spirit symbolized by the Eagle. He was also found in the Constellation of the Great Bear – and one figure has the bear leaning on the Eagle's breast. The Greeks believed the Great Bear kept watch over the Universe. The American Indians believe that the bear is immortal, and reincarnates into another bear body. This same belief is found among the Ainu of Saghalien Island in Japan.

The ancients thought that the number five was sacred to the God of Light, who was sometimes symbolized by a bull with five horns.

The mystic armies of the sky were grouped into units typified by oxen, sheep, and geese. The starry hosts, recruited from earth, were believed to fight everlastingly against evil. Legends of this contest can be found in many cultures.

In Babylon, the leader of the hosts was Merodach, a name that meant *steer*. He was known as the "troubler of the evil one." As King of the hosts he was identified with Jupiter. According to the Babylonians, Jupiter was the tender of the stars and Merodach pastured the gods like sheep. Merodach was also responsible for passing out duties to the star souls. He made the moon shine and that made him ruler of the night. He was thus associated with the moon god Sin – the light-producer. *Sin* is the origin of Mt. Sinai. He was symbolized as a mighty steer with strong horns and limbs.

In India, the leader of the star souls was Indra. He was the god with ten thousand eyes. He was the watcher and Lord of the Stars.

The Persians had a supreme being named Ormuz who was the protector of man and fought with evil spirits. The part man played in the struggle was important – the prize was his soul.

The Greeks and Romans had Jupiter as their savior against the forces of darkness. Scandinavians called their being Thor, and he was a dragonslayer.

HOUSE
The house stands for nourishment and protection, so it is thus feminine and connected to Mother Earth.

I

Iris
Ivory

IRIS
The white iris is a symbol of the Virgin Mary.

IVORY
In antique times, ivory was as prized as gold. It was considered a rare gem as a result of two qualities: its color, white, which symbolized purity, and its hardness, which the early Christians likened to moral strength and the body of Jesus in the tomb.

The most important quality of ivory is its unchangeability. Gold and silver may be melted and molded into other forms, and precious stones may be reset, thus making new ornaments. But ivory, once it has been carved into an object, cannot be changed. This factor made an impression on ancient movements in the arts. As ivory moved from country to country it inspired new art forms and valuable sculptures.

In the seventeenth century, Sir Thomas Browne referred to a fantasy concerning ivory. All of our dreams were said to pass through a gate wrought of ivory and one of horn. The dreams that passed through the gate of ivory were delusional dreams. Those that passed through the gate of horn always came true.

J

Jade
Justica

JADE

Jade is a stone of healing that is said to have mystical medicinal value. Colic Stone (used to heal children's colic) by Spanish explorers was, in actuality, Nephrite. Ritually it was said to have qualities of solar light – thus its heavenly relationship. Jade was a stone worthy of the Son of Heaven, the Emperor. The hardness of the stone made it a symbol of eternity.

The Chinese judge jade for its color, delicacy, and freedom from cracks and other imperfections. It should have a greasy appearance when polished. The stones that feel dry are not as perfect as the "greasy" ones.

Jadeite, which comes in lavender and bright greens, is brighter and more colorful than Nephrite.

There are those who argue there was never a Stone Age in China, but scholars have found jade spearheads and other weapons made in the crude manner of the Paleolithic Age. The earliest carvings from the Shang-Tin Dynasty (1766–1122 B.C.) are sophisticated.

Those from the Chou Dynasty (c. 1000 B.C.) are found in objects used in ritual ceremonies. The Chinese held jade in high esteem even then, and carved it for religious purposes. The Chinese used jade vessels for sacrifices to their ancestors.

During the Han Dynasty, Confusionism, Taoism, and Buddhism became the three religions of China. They're so linked that they have one main principle, but with individual superstitions particular to a sect or locality. In the mix was animism – the power of nature spirits, genii, and deified heros.

Jade was believed to be endowed with supernatural powers, and was found in the emperor's court in the form of paraphernalia used by fortunetellers and advisers. It was used in seances wherein soothsayers foretold the future of their country. The Chinese became wrapped up in jade lore and deemed jade the symbol of sovereignty and Divine History.

The Ming Dynasty featured jade carvings that reflected both the tranquil and warlike periods of that dynasty. Jade carvings reflected the religious and superstitious ideas prevalent during the Dynasty.

JUSTICA

This is the famous goddess of Justice and Law who sometimes represents various parts of the United States government. She holds a sword to punish the guilty, a scale for weighing the evidence, and she is blindfolded to denote impartiality.

K

Keys
Kings

KEYS

The key symbolizes mastery and is also the symbol of housewifery. In classic times, the Roman marriage ceremony included giving the bride a key.

In Denmark, a key represents secrets, and the chamberlains of the courts there wear a key as part of their regalia.

Receiving the key to a city is a traditional honor. Today we still honor our citizen guests with keys.

Gibraltar, the city at the crossroads of the Mediterranean, has a key in its coat of arms, as do Geneva and Osten.

The keys of Heaven, held by St. Peter, indicate whether a soul is to be sent to Hell or Heaven.

Keys are very important to the Catholic Church, and two crossed keys are part of the coat of arms of the papacy.

KINGS

In early times the king behaved symbolically when it came to religion and his relationship with the god being worshipped in his city. The kings used language as well as signs, monuments, and buildings to symbolize their importance. Special ceremonial forms were used as well. His behavior toward his subjects and the gods served to give him the power of the Divine Right of Kings, and he collected taxes and tributes as a result. The decoration of buildings with murals and reliefs varied in topical content. They showed the king in warlike array and depicted his exploits. There were pictures of the king meeting with the gods.

The Assyrian rulers from 721 to 627 B.C. were specially equipped with these paintings. The fame of the kings spread through the Near East, and some were feared and respected more than others – through the greatness of their deeds – and the symbolic building and paintings representing them.

L

LADDERS

Ladders are straightforward and bring you to God or another higher plain. The biblical symbol of Jacob's Ladder represents the movement of souls from Earth to Heaven. Before Adam (and the fall from grace with God) there was a ladder that brought souls to and fro; this ladder won't be available again until the Second Coming. St. John Climacus said of the ladder that each rung represented a good deed that put a soul that much closer to God.

Beside religious symbolism, the ladder stands for moving upward in intellect or character. Intellectual striving means self-improvement and perfection.

LAMB

In the Bible, the lamb was the animal of sacrifice and therefore of suffering. It was also sacrificed in the Greek days of Apollonic temples, where its blood was used for purposes of divination and prophecy.

The lamb became the symbol of innocence being persecuted. The lamb was characterized by meekness when under attack by wolves, and the lamb came to symbolize Christ as the Redeemer.

John the Baptist characterized Christ as "The Lamb of God which taketh away the sins of the world." The lamb is much in evidence in Christian art through the ages. In Christian paintings, the lamb carries a cross and stands on a hillside from which four streams of water flow. The hill symbolizes the House of God, and the four streams are the four Holy Gospels flowing as the Word of God toward the earth.

Sometimes the lamb appears in distress when portraying Jesus as the Good Shepherd, but the distressed lamb also stands for a sinner.

LANGUAGE

The Welsh language resembles Sanskrit more than the language of other European countries. The Gaelic language, too, has Sanskrit letters and words.

The Welsh language is designed to include abstract thought and physics. Welsh is suited to oratory, in fact more so than English. It has broad vowels and no hissing sound to interrupt its sonorous flow.

Bengal is also an euphonious language. It's related to Sanskrit, which has the melody of Italian and the Germanic ability to express complex thought. Grammar is important to the Hindus.

According to the Celts, music and literature have a divine origin. The Sanskrit *Vani*, meaning *word*, is a symbol of the Goddess of Learning, personified by Saravati.

In the ancient times, the Celts did not use last names. Even today, among the Hindus, surnames are sometimes missing. They aren't considered a necessity as they are in the West. The names of Hindus are often gods or goddesses. Celts can also trace their names back to the gods.

LOCUSTS

Locusts are a symbol of destruction, and they still work together in swarms to eat crops and trees.

Pharaoh was plagued by locusts, and God threatened Israel with a plague of locusts for its disobedience. In the final days of the world, an army of locusts will prepare for the final battle. They will wear gold crowns on their heads and they have men's faces. Their hair is like a woman's, and their teeth are like a lion's teeth. The sound of their wings is as many horses in battle.

Pharaoh's daughter used magic to attract King Solomon. She used red thread and three locusts that she made into her magical charm of seduction.

A gold locust was the symbol of Apollo, the sun god. Perhaps it was chosen to warn against drought and the sun's hot rays that dry vegetation.

In the days of Queen Elizabeth I, the locust was used in stone decorations for the Royal Exchange. It may have been in commemoration of Lord Gresham, the founder, whose crest contained the locust. It has remained to this day as a symbol for goldsmiths and for London bankers in honor of Lord Gresham.

LOTUS

The lotus is a symbol of fertility and it represents the intellect and material, worldly items. The white lotus represents Saravati, the goddess of learning. Brahma is symbolized by the pink lotus – or the dawn. Blue lotuses are associated with Vishnu and fertility.

The lotus appears in the craftsmanship of the Picts from ancient times in Scotland; it also appeared in the drawings of the Maya.

Images of the Mother Goddess and the Great Father were made by craftsmen doing their best work. These were religious symbols – and in architecture, sculpture, and painting – they made the images for the homes of the people. Only the rich built temples with all the appointments, including artwork and icons.

Siva's symbol is a linga and may be found at Aurangabad. At this temple, the lotus – which surrounds buildings dedicated in Vishnu – is of perfect construction.

Only Western scholars call the worship of the lingam icon worship. The lotus is known as the padma in ancient Indian culture. This motif shows up on the pillars of temples as the female element on the male pillar. Together they make the creative principal of life.

The lotus is sometimes known as the flower of marriage. It means that the fruition of the earth contains the seed of all creation. The Celtic lotus leaf in the Cathedral of Iona follows the Aryan (from India) conception.

M

MALE AND FEMALE SYMBOLS

The sperm symbol (a circle with an arrow pointing from it) is the symbol for male and the cross with a loop (the ankh) for female. The symbols show up in astronomy, too, where they stand for  the planets Mars and Venus. In engineering, they represent iron and copper. In the Middle Ages, astronomers (who were also astrologers) used the symbols in the horoscopes they drew up. Hence the symbols lingered in astronomy as the signs of Mars and Venus – war and love. The god Mars used iron in his war weapons and so iron was associated with Mars. As for the female symbol, Venus entered the world at Cyprus, known for its copper. So copper became associated with Venus. Mars and Venus were regarded as stereotypes of maleness and femaleness, so their symbols took on the meaning of male and female. Today the female symbol is used by the womens' liberation movement, sometimes depicted with a fist in the loop of the female sign.

MAYPOLE

The maypole is as celebrated among the Hindus as it is in England. It represents the sexual union honoring the Hindu cupid. The Hindu festival went on for three months in Medieval times.

In Edinburgh the Maypole was set up in the street at the south door of the church, and, once in place, was higher than the steeple. On May 1 at 4 A.M., maypole dancers would collect, wearing brilliant colors, and dance around the pole until dawn. This was construed as a fertility rite. Rites relating to phallicism have appeared in South Asia, Southeastern Europe, and North Africa.

Some Western scholars have called this worship obscene, and quote sacred Hindu scripture to show it was condemned. But Eastern scholars say that Western ones just don't understand Eastern scripture. Lust and self-indulgence are deemed obscene in Eastern scripture. The Vedic scriptures teach that nature worship is blessed.

MEDICINE

Before Hippocrates came along in Greece as the father of Western medicine, the Hindus had built an extensive pharmacopoeia and wrote treatises on medical and surgical subjects. The Hindu pharmacopoeia was solidified by Chanvantari, the father of Hindu medicine. Today, the Hindus are wary of surgery – as they believe it destroys the nervous system.

The Mayans knew of the surgical procedures used by the Hindus.

Among the Celts the profession of physician was passed on from father to son.

The caduceus is a symbol of medicine today.

MERCURY

The Romans thought of Mercury (the Greek Hermes) as the guide and the "Great Mare." Here the caduceus is decorated by a winged horse or mare.

The magic wand that Mercury used to put people to sleep or wake them up was the white-ribboned staff – the caduecus. The symbols of Mercury were a lizard and a cock, and his animal sacrifice was a pregnant sow.

Among the Greeks, Hermes was the god of good luck and dice. This herald of Heaven was the conductor of souls, like Christ and the Egyptian god Anubis.

In Britain, Mercury was the pagan god of Ways. Statues to Mercury were erected at roadside crossings, especially at the junction of three roads. Thousands of Celtic markers are still in place. Among the Celts, Mercury was also the god of Merchants, and marketplaces were denoted by a cross.

MILK
Milk, sometimes associated with purity, is an important symbol of fertility, life, and abundance. It's also a symbol of great goodness, and its absence indicates suffering. The concept of a land of milk and honey is a concept of abundance, being blessed by God. God promised to lead the Israelites into such a land of abundance when they came out of Egypt.

The land of milk and honey was also where the Golden Race under Cronus lived without pain or work, eating of the fruits of the earth.

Another myth speaks of how the Milky Way came to be. It was born when the goddess Rhea gave birth to Zeus and splattered her milk across the heavens.

In early magical rites, fertility was wrought by spells designed to bring milk to women and cattle.

Throughout the Middle Ages, every witch was thought to have a familiar given to her by the devil. It might be a toad or a cat, and a witch would feed it with milk from a third teat made under her arm by the devil. During witch hunts these marks were looked for, and many innocent people were put to death as a result of having one.

MIRROR
Japanese mythology relates that the Sun goddess, upon leaving her grandchild, gave him a mirror and told him that when he looked in the mirror, he would see her. The mirror is regarded as a symbol of knowledge by the Japanese.

MOON
Moon worship is older than sun worship. The moon god of the Assyrians, Sin, is a god of wisdom. The Egyptian god, Thoth, is a god of learning. And Tanuanpat, the ancient moon god of India, was supposed to be self-created. He was the child of himself.

A moon god was often symbolic of summer. Summer was thought to be the unifying season. It separated spring (the time of planting) and autumn (the time of fathering the crops). The harvest moon ripens the fields.

The Egyptians believed the moon god to actually be a goddess – mother of the world. She had a male and female makeup because she was impregnated by the sun, and then scattered her seed upon the earth.

There is a tie between moon, earth, and water worship – as all three are feminine in nature. It was actually thought that moon rays on the crops were more beneficial than the sun's rays.

The moon was thought to be the source of all water. Blood and sap were included and the moon controlled these.

The proponents of Ea – the Sumerian god of water, earth, and heaven – believed that the very essence of life was in water. Blood was the essence of life and the worship of water was connected to the belief that the blood of a god flowed in these sacred waters. Sap, in India, was thought to be the blood of the trees.

The idea was, in ancient religions, that sins could not be expiated without the flow of blood. And in these ancient religions expiation was thought to come from drinking blood. The idea was prevalent in Mexico.

The sacrament of eating bread and drinking wine in religious ceremonies was the partaking of the blood and flesh of the gods of productivity. The idea that we are sanctified by partaking of the blood (wine) and flesh (bread) goes back to prehistory. This symbolic act was amalgamated into Christian worship and continues today. This actually comes from nature worship.

Eventually the belief of the supremacy of the moon over the sun gave way to the idea that they had a common birth and were essentially one being – overall and supreme. The sun was the male principle, and the moon was the female sustenance principle.

Thus the Egyptians called their generative gods – the sun and the moon – Isis and Osiris. These two produced all life on earth. The sun showed the moon the ways of generation while she in turn inseminated the earth and elements. A sun disk resting on a crescent moon symbolized the conjunction of the sun and the moon.

Plutarch wrote in *On the Face of the Moon* that good souls remain on the moon and enjoy perfect harmony there. They work to regulate the affairs of earth and serve mankind. Some symbols of the time show a half moon face scrunched up in a frown.

The moon symbolized the celestial Mother. And the crescent moon is a symbol of virginity, and is the sign of Diana and, in Christian belief, the Virgin Mary. The crescent moon was also a symbol of the Lord of Heaven and may be found in the Catacombs.

MORALITY PLAYS
Morality plays are allegories – abstract ideas symbolized in a personal form.

MYSTICISM
Mystics in the 1500s were tracked down and murdered. Witches met similar fates, but the mystics believed in God and had enormous faith. A crucifix made of three bent spikes and a nail is a symbol that the mystics adopted. It was the symbol of a Man of Sorrows. They were known, by some authors, as the true Christians.

The devil spat on the mystics and brought them unbounding troubles. Some wore caps with bells and played the Fool. It is true that God's wisdom was ignored and the devil reigned in those years.

But the mystics were content. When they were laughed at, they ignored their ridiculers. In fact, they gloried in the tortures – they belonged to God, after all. Their watchword – so they might know each other – was "not to please the world." They also said that people who did not suffer gladly for Christ did not fully understand the spirit of Christ.

The Fool's cap was a symbol of gladly suffering wrongs. They were fools for Christ's sake. Being reviled, they blessed the accuser. Being persecuted, they endured it. The mystics wrote widely of being a fool for Christ. St. Francis of Assisi called them troubadours of God. The troubadours fanned opinions against Rome, according to some authors of the time. The symbol of the Medieval fool was a cockscomb guarded between two horns.

The word *Silly* originally meant simple and innocent. This translates down to the symbol Fire of God Almighty. Among the Mexicans the fool is posed in a "house of fire."

The personal symbol of the fool is the simpleton's house as a hoop, eye, or circle.

Symbolism has been described as the language of the angels. To the mystics scattered throughout Europe from Germany to Spain, and from Italy to Sweden, symbolism was the language of the invisible Church. And the mystics used symbols to communicate with each other.

N

Names
Numbers
Numbers in Birthdays
More Numbers

6
9
27
23
4
7
17
2
234
1
97
3
9
43
5

NAMES

The last name Baldwin comes from the Celtic god Balder. The Irish last name Ram comes from the Indian name Rama. There's a Ram's Island off County Wexford in Ireland. There was also a Rama tribe in South America.

The name Pulomar may be linked to the English name Pulman.

Morris is a last name as well as a style of dance, and might have evolved from the Maruts of whom Indra, King of the gods, is the leader. Morris Dancers employ symbols such as a mirror, ribbons, and bells. The church at Abbot's Bromley, which is dedicated to St. Nicholas, has a connection with the Maruts through the symbol of the deer.

The Druids divided themselves into three sections, one of which was the Physicians. These doctors were named Vaids – which may be compared to the Indian word, Vaidja, which is even today what Indian physicians are called. Sifka, in mythology, is named Vaidyanath, which is Lord of the Physicians.

NUMBERS

Favorite numbers throughout the world are 2, 3, and 5. Three is a favorite of English and German people. Mediterranean people choose 2, and 5 is favored by Chinese people. India favors the number 2; 7 is also an occult number there, and 7 is a favorite with Russians. The Spanish prefer 19 (a double number). In Mexico the number to consider lucky is 17. In Hawaii the number of choice is 13. These preferences are deeply embedded in the cultures of these people and influence their daily lives.

Numbers represent the vibrations found in nature. They're occult and sometimes show off nature in its cyclic guise. Here are some metaphysical interpretations of numbers:

The number *1* symbolizes unity, will, life, maleness, reason, and logic. It stands for law and order, and it has a positive vibration.

The number 2 symbolizes duality, duty, friendliness, negativity, diplomacy. It is contrast and change.

The number 3 symbolizes love, wisdom, pregnancy, versatility. It's one's opposite, and provides perfection in art and inspiration.

The number 4 symbolizes justice, mercy, strength, prudence, solidity, opinionatedness. Represents the man of character carrying the triad of divinity.

The number 5 symbolizes the bridge in nature between the higher and lower selves. With 5 we touch matter in its different planes. It is psychic yet rational, representing the unconquerable power over God's world of matter. Five symbolizes these with concrete thought patterns as well as theory and practice.

The number 6 symbolizes effort, combat, indecision, and activity in these areas. It represents the ability to see both sides of a problem or argument. But it can't make decisions easily. It is the opposition of emotion and rationality.

The number 7 symbolizes perfection of form on all planes during our particular age. Seven symbolizes victory, perfection, analysis. Life's lessons are analyzed. Seven is nature's basic number. Our bodies have seven parts – head, chest, abdomen, two legs, and two arms.

The number 8 symbolizes power, growth, struggle. It stands for the law of evolution – also cause and effect, as well as standing for Karma. Eight separates the sheep from the wolves.

The number 9 symbolizes grounding, can't be moved. Prudence is a quality of 9. It's becoming of self, self-control, energy. The negative side is rebelliousness and doubt.

The number 10 symbolizes ruling the world, unity, and sharing.

The number 13 symbolizes justice, resurrection, initiative, creativity, and understanding.

The number 17 is a symbol of victory, self-expression, and power.

The number 19 represents force, circumspection, testing – and people are either fortunate or not so – according to their 19 qualities.

NUMBERS IN BIRTHDAYS

First day of the month: Indicates a person who will, in life, learn self-expression. Understands unity and self-reliance. These people should avoid habits and addictions which are especially hard to get rid of.

Second day of the month: These people are peace-makers and philosophers. Diplomats are born on the second day.

Third day of the month: This person will have the need to be spiritual, and needs to learn harmony of mind and body. His or her lower self will give in to the spiritual side. Their creativity shouldn't be hidden but expressed.

Fourth day of the month: These people are dependable and hard workers. They're honest souls and are spiritual.

Fifth day of the month: The senses are important to these people. They should be used carefully. They will have clear-headedness and insight, and a chaotic imagination.

Sixth day of the month: These people know the difference between reality and unreality. They know how to oppose and conquer. They are victorious over the lower self. They love beauty and must learn to balance life.

Seventh day of the month: These people should learn reasoning in school. They should grow spiritually and mentally, and should pay attention to the inner voice and learn life well.

Eighth day of the month: These people symbolize poise and balance. They have the spiritual and material world in harmony. They are adept at finances.

Ninth day of the month: These people think about their next life and prepare for it. They balance the spiritual and material. They're good at the occult because they know how to concentrate their energies. They are often philanthropists.

Tenth day of the month: These people are born again. They continually graduate from one plateau to the next.

Eleventh day of the month: These people are adept at fixing things that come apart. They take what's broken and redo it until it works. This is the way that such people serve God.

Twelfth day of the month: Such people gain Heaven through service to others.

Thirteenth day of the month: These people must overcome all ill and turn it into virtue. They must practice being merciful and moral. When they do, they attain victory of the higher self.

Fourteenth day of the month: These people are full of initiative, dependability, and are independent.

Fifteenth day of the month: This birth date indicates the need to become an independent thinker, and to extract life's lessons from experience. These people are often teachers.

Sixteenth day of the month: These people need to exercise willpower and independence and overcome obstacles as they choose between opposites.

Seventeenth day of the month: These people are often teachers, as those born on this day they must give forth self-expression. They are introspective people and symbolize the power of synthesis.

Eighteenth day of the month: These people must develop willpower and learn to be alone. They're usually financial experts and become rich through integrity in financial fields.

Nineteenth day of the month: These people will learn lessons from the past and become highly spiritual. If spirituality is attained, a new life is gained. It's like moving from one world to another. A lower self dies young, but a higher self may live forever.

Twentieth day of the month: These people make good health professionals. They are kindly and capable of giving spiritual enlightenment. They embody national service.

Twenty-first day of the month: These people are takers and need spiritual guidance. They need to learn the art of being a self-starter.

Twenty-second day of the month: These people are in transition and are learning spirituality. They make good ministers, rabbis, or priests when they evolve. They sometimes make good doctors, but their primary bent is the church or synagogue.

Twenty-third day of the month: Service to many people is the watchword of these people. They, too, may become members of the clergy.

Twenty-fourth day of the month: These people make good judges. They are also good soldiers if born on this day. They must learn endurance and faith if born on this day.

Twenty-fifth day of the month: These people become diplomats or CIA agents. They are unselfish and give of themselves without question.

Twenty-sixth day of the month: These people make good generals and military brass. They live to serve and are attuned to conquering.

Twenty-seventh day of the month: These people make excellent psychiatrists or psychologists. They love to serve people and help others who are depressed or otherwise mentally disabled.

Twenty-eighth day of the month: Cult leaders are sometimes born on the twenty-eighth. They show others the way to the Divine Plan that they understand.

Twenty-ninth day of the month: Presidents are among those born on this day. World leaders of every sort give universal service to others.

Thirtieth day of the Month: These people are artists – musicians and painters. They produce art for others to enjoy, not just for themselves.

Thirty-first day of the month: These people are artists too, but must learn initiative and discipline. They need to become spiritual too, not just creative with form.

MORE NUMBERS

The ancients believed that numbers, as symbols, revealed the divine order of the universe. Pythagoras, in the sixth century b.c., made a system out of numbers, believing that numbers constituted the essence of things. He believed that Heaven was a musical scale (the music of the planets and stars). Numbers, under Pythagoras' system, were divided into odd and even, one and many, straight and curved. The balance of the universe was brought about by the relationship of opposites: 1, 3, 5, 7, 9 were Heavenly numbers, and 2, 4, 6, 8, and 10 were earth numbers. Pythagoras also invented the octave in music.

Numbers are symbols, and some of their meanings follow:

1. Represents unity and origin. Identified with reason.

2. Signifies male and female. Two is itself regarded as a female number, and a negative symbol.

3. Symbolizes creation and resurrection, the trinity. The number three itself represents music, geometry, and astronomy.

4. The root of all things, the basis of nature and a perfect number. Symbolizes cubes and squares. Associated with justice because it signifies that it's a product of equals.

5. Represents marriage, as it's a union of male and female numbers – three and two.

6. Symbolizes competition (God created the world in six days). Also, the Star of David has six points as do the Chakras (the wheel of Vishnu). There's a myth that the world will be divided into six ages and that destruction will be followed by the bringing in of a new age.

Pythagoras believed six represented the perfection of all forms. Six is the most important number in the ancients' calendars. Six symbolizes family and work as creative energy.

7. An important number to the ancients is seven. Pythagoras called it the vehicle of life. It contains the triangle and square (female and male symbols), therefore, it represents the body and soul.

In the Bible, the symbol of seven means the holy day. It's the number of religion. It's the number of life because premature babies born in the seventh month live, while those born in the eighth month usually die.

8. Symbolizes elevation to a higher life and the deliverance from today's evils. The ancients' circle of life had seven bands, and the eighth was with God. In Jewish lore, eight is associated with cleaning and purification.

Eight people were saved by Noah's Ark. Eight is connected with the Deluge (in Chinese traditions) and is important in cosmogony. It's a holy number.

9. Associated with failure and defeat of character, because it's one short of the perfect ten. It's looked upon as an evil number as it's an upside-down six. It's also the number of mankind, as pregnancy is usually nine months. It's also identified with the ocean and the horizon as limitless power.

10. Denotes completion and the end. Pythagoras thought of it as the perfect number. It represents God, man, and the universe because it contains the four prime numbers, including all math and musical projections, and defines the system of the world.

Pythagoras used ten to symbolize age, power, and faith. They divided the heavenly planets into ten orbits.

Oak Tree
Owl

OAK TREE

Among all the trees, the oak is the symbol of strength. Oaks appear in many military symbols. Oak leaves are part of the badge worn by American and German soldiers. In England, trials were sometimes held beneath a towering oak. And in America, the oak is the state tree for six states.

OWLS

The owl was the symbol of the goddess Athena in Greece, and Minerva in Rome. Athena, the goddess of war, was the strategy planner and a master of tactics. She was also the goddess of wisdom. Owls used to inhabit Athens by the tens of thousands – the owl even appeared on their coins. The owl became associated with Athens and wisdom. It's a bookstore symbol in Denmark.

The owl is often thought of as the harbinger of death as it comes out at night. In the Renaissance it appeared in artworks as sleep and death symbols.

P

PEACE SIGN

The sign is a semaphore signal connoting the letters N and D, which stand for Nuclear Disarmament. While it was originally a symbol advocating nuclear disarmament groups, it grew to stand for pacifism in general, and on occasion for opposition to "the Establishment."

PEARL

Because it's hidden in a shell, the pearl – born of heaven and the sea – represents a valuable mystic center, just as the soul is more precious than the body that holds it.

There were eulogies to the sacred power of the pearl in ancient Vedic hymns. In them it is sung that the bones of the gods turn to pearl. Used as an amulet, the pearl protects the body from all harm.

The Chinese believed the pearl to be a symbol of fertility. The oyster, it was said, helped in childbirth.

The Greeks and Romans, who wore lots of amulets, prized the pearl and thought that it had occult powers. It was said to bring luck in love and guard marriage.

The pearl was used as medicine in ancient China and elsewhere. It was said to be a cure for madness, fever, and jaundice.

With the advent of Christianity, the pearl became a symbol of salvation. In one parable, Jesus mentioned the pearl of great price, exchanged for all he had by a pearl merchant.

The pearl is a symbol of truth, and it is often displayed as a symbol of wealth.

Cleopatra is said to have drunk a pearl mixed in wine to impress Mark Antony.

PENTACLE

The pentacle, with which King Solomon performed white magic, was sometimes called the Seal of Solomon. When placed right-side up, the pentacle was a powerful amulet for good but, when inverted, it was a symbol of black magic.

Today it's very common in certain parts of the world. In astrology it represents the five planets.

PHOENIX

Historically, tales of the phoenix appeared in ancient Egypt and Arabian countries. The Phoenix lives a thousand years, then goes to the desert, builds a fire, leaps in, and rises again to live another thousand years. Only one phoenix exists in the world at a time. For ancient Christians it was a symbol of Immaculate Conception and of the Resurrection. In the Garden of Eden, the phoenix rejected the snake's (devil's) wily way to eat the fruit of knowledge, and therefore gained eternal life.

In Classic times, the phoenix symbolized eternity.

The phoenix was the alchemical symbol of fire.

The phoenix was a symbol on the flag of Greece under Papadopopulos.

PIGS

Pigs are charming when they're young. And yet we know the epithet "pig" is derogatory. We all remember Napoleon from *Animal Farm*. And Shakespeare even wrote of pigs. When left in the wilderness, pigs are clean. It is only in the sty that they're odoriferous.

Rembrandt, Reubens, and Gainsborough (to name a few painters) depicted the pig. And statues of pigs may be found in churches (around pulpits and benches) and cathedrals. Here they play musical instruments and other such activities.

From earliest childhood, we know the rhyme of "this little pig went to market, this little pig stayed home . . ."

The earliest picture of a pig yet discovered – of a wild boar attacking – was painted some 40,000 years ago in the caves of Altamira, Spain. Archaeologists presume the animals depicted there were believed to be magical and gave hunters influence over their quarry.

Rock paintings of boars have been found in Rhodesia, and there is a well-known one in Scotland. Christians portrayed the pig as the symbol of the seven deadly sins, including fornication, greed, and gluttony. Many examples of carved pigs may be found in churches in England dating from the 14th and 15th centuries.

The boar also appears on the inside walls of St. David's Cathedral in South Wales, and is in a part that is the oldest. The Picts of the Orkneys had a boar as an emblem. Since the Picts spoke Norn and not Gaelic, it seems the boar came from another source.

There are many boar symbols in Scotland and Ireland. Sometimes the boar is carved in stone above a grave, usually for a hero. At St. Andrew's Church, in Cumberland, there are four gravestones bearing the boar. These boars have braided manes.

Modern-day pigs in church are based on the medieval models and are associated with St. Anthony, the patron saint of swine. There's a pig on Henry VIII's tomb that represented St. Anthony.

In Oxford, at Christ Church Cathedral, there is an image of St. Frideswine, who is depicted in a sty. And in the twentieth century church in Frilsham, Berkshire, the sow and piglets tell the story of the founding of the church by St. Brannock and St. Guthloe.

Pigs show up in British heraldry as well as churches. The Bacon family has a boar in its heraldry. Another boar is in the Kirky Church near Lincoln, symbolizing John Wildbore.

The annual pig kill is represented in churches too. In Kent, England, the symbolized kill is in November. And in southern Europe, the scenes attribute the boar kill to October and even September, depending on the weather. In France, the picture is a carving showing the actual pig kill going on.

Sometimes the pig represented the tithe – that the pig was one-tenth of a man's worldly goods belonging to the Church.

It's sometimes suggested that the sow and piglets symbolized lust, greed, and other such defects of character, and that they are used as a warning sign. In the Bestierie, a book of beasts, pigs symbolized sinners and heretics. The boar also symbolized evil princes. In Norwich, there's a depiction of the seven deadly sins. An angry figure rides a wild boar symbolizing anger and passion – while in another depiction the boar is ridden by a drunkard representing greed. Carved and painted jousters (mounted on boars) may have been satires of the tournaments of the times.

Misericords, or bench ends, were often carved in churches, and the pig assumed importance in these carvings. One famed carving is of a pig wearing cowls and preaching to Reynard the Fox. This was a symbol of the hatred born of the Abbot Glastonbury of the time. Henry VIII had on his stationery a watermark of a hog wearing a tiara, showing his contempt for the Pope. A musical pig playing bagpipes appears in carvings all over Europe. And another pig plays the harp. The pig as musician was meant to portray the vagabond or wandering minstrel.

In the Muslim and Jewish religions, the pig is seen as filthy. But to the Greeks and Romans the pig symbolized fertility. It was used as an offering to a number of gods and goddesses, like Cybsis, Diane, and Ceres. To the Romans, the boar symbolized strength and fearlessness, and it became a military symbol. Part of the uniform of the Roman Twentieth Legion was an amulet representing a wild boar.

PILGRIMS

The Puritans were known in the Middle Ages as the "pure ones." A unicorn feeding on a fleur-de-lis (an emblem of the Holy Trinity) is one of the few surviving symbols of this Chris-

tian heritage. Sometimes it is seen with a cross and again is seen with the letters IS, which stands for Jesus the Salvator.

Printers were important in the early times, and printer John Day adopted as his motto "Arise, for it is day." Sometimes the light symbol was a candlestick, often with a cross – or the letter X – which is a starcross.

Some designs were just for Christ. One such symbol is three locks of hair – or Christ's oneness with the Trinity.

God was represented as a shield – Jesus as a fish. This was an early Christian symbol frequently found in the Catacombs. Often the fish is a dolphin, which has always been regarded as a friend of mankind. To the Greeks, the Dolphin was a savior of the shipwrecked. Thence it became a symbol to early Christians.

Halos circling the head represent man's travel between wretchedness and perfection. "Only the perfect can bring an thing to perfecton," said scholar Eckactshausen. Christ is the only one who can open our eyes. Jesus is the savior of many – bringing them from darkness to the light. Ignorance falls from our eyes in the presence of Jesus' light.

One of the Pilgrims learned from Christ that it was necessary to be born again. The Christ informed the Pilgrim that he had to revisit the spots in his life where he had gone astray. He enters a church called Christianity and watches as people pass by the curtained and screened chancel. The pilgrim goes to it immediately and perceives it as the truth of Christianity.

POMEGRANATE
The pomegranate, a favorite fruit in the Middle East, is a symbol of fertility and unity.

In Greek mythology, the pomegranate is associated with immortality and resurrection, and with the goddess Persephone – who was abducted to the Greek hell, or Hades – and whose periodic return to earth is symbolic of springtime. Adonis was conceived by Nana, who ate a pomegranate seed.

The Egyptian Sekhmet, who was a wild woman soldier, was also associated with the pomegranate. When Ra saw her slaughtering all the men on the battlefield, he despaired of the human race and made a magic potion of pomegranate juice – which he put in seven thousand jugs. Sekhmet mistook the red juice for blood and drank it, becoming too drunk to go on with her slaughter, and thus saving mankind.

In the Bible, the pomegranate decorated the robes of the High Priest in the temple which Solomon built in Jerusalem. In European Judaic tradition, the menorah is surmounted by a Star of David. But originally, it was a pomegranate as a symbol of rain, and the seeds stood for the many children of Israel. It is also true of the pomegranate that worms won't touch it, so it is symbolic of indestructibility.

PREHISTORIC SYMBOLS

The crescent in the coat of arms of the University of St. Andrew is not a Christian symbol. It's a symbol of the great Aryan mother, but appears on the continent as the Christian Madonna and Child.

Coins have been located in the Cornish area of Karn Bri. They're inscribed with the goddess Kerridwen. The half-moon is the ark on cosmic waters.

In the ancient past, colors were significant. The Picts tattooed themselves blue and white, a symbolic connection attaching to the colors of the great Mahamaya in her incarnation as Night.

The churchyard at St. Briage in Cornwall is round, and egg-shaped stones can be found there. They're natural stones and not carved, but were brought from the beach where they were chosen for their shape.

The Druids were adept at many and various arts, from coloring their pottery to knowing how to make themselves invisible. Perhaps not many Druids knew how to shape-change, but it was known and done.

The Land of the Sidhe was a mental training place for those who wished to be adepts in India. Adepts could assume an imperceptable form – becoming invisible. This is the Sidhe training, which is called Anima. In Celtic legend, the Land of the Sidhe became the home of elves and fairies, and the poet, Shelley, is thought to have been an adept and achieved invisibility. Peridur was given a precious stone in the Land of Sidhe which made him invisible. King Arthur had a tartan that did the same thing.

After Christianity came, all magic and sorcery was thought to be evil.

When the Saxons came to London, it was the center of black magic. But the effects of the magic frightened the Saxons and they left London for some time.

The art of invisibility was used in Edinburgh to good effect. The story goes that a doctor had a housekeeper, a

Celt. The woman was fond of him. As he was getting ready to go to a poor section of town, his housekeeper begged him not to go, as second sight came to her and warned of impending danger. As he decided to go anyway, the house-keeper told him that he would be able to see but not be seen in that district.

The doctor found the house he was going to. A woman answered the door and, looking at him, cried "Who's there?" She then saw the doctor and they went indoors. The people of the house were gathered around an old man in bed. The doctor perceived that he had been called to hurry death to the old man. He used invisibility and withdrew, then pondered his new powers, which he proceeded to develop.

Firewalking was also prevalent in those days. At a church in Lych Gate there's an arrangement of stones for firewalking. There are bars of stones that were used in the ceremony at that site.

Ancient people amused themselves with numerous festivals. There were solar and lunar festivals. Calendars were kept, and those that resemble each other belonged to the Hindus, the American Indians, British, French Bretons, and the Indians at San Juan Capistrano. The Celtic Land of the Sidhe corresponds to the Land of Siddha in India.

The Tuatha, who were British people with magical powers, could appear and disappear at will (were these people space aliens?). This power was eventually subdued by later people who pooh-poohed it. There are still some traces of the power, but nothing organized.

The Fairy Cross in Somerset is a reminder of the fairies who inhabited the area. They were known in Scotland, Ireland, the British Isles, and Brittany.

The Siddhas are people who have attained Siddhi. These are superhuman powers reached through the practice of Yoga. Anima is the power of reducing one's size – becoming practically invisible – and this power may have belonged to the fairies of mythology.

Agni of Siva's family, the spirit of Fire, or the Sacred Tree, or pillar of flame – and the mantra for the drink which fuels the flames are all highly symbolic. The *Vedas*, the oldest classical writing of the Aryan Hindus, teach that fire is the originator of all life on the planet. But that fire is helpless to produce life unless it's united with water (the moon), so that the sun and the moon (fire and water) are held in myth to be the parents of creation.

Angi, the fire god, has inspired the best hymns in literature. His beautiful face is painted by artists, and he is represented as the Rising Sun. He has a beard and holds a water carrier in his left hand: in his right hand he holds a rosary. His figure appears in a halo of flames and is sitting on a seat made of the half-moon.

PRIESTHOOD

A privileged group of people, potential Druids went into the priesthood to study religion and mysticism. The priests and lawmakers were the important figures in this society. There were scientists and bards who committed history to memory.

During today's Gorsedad festivals you can see the sections of the Druid community. They wear robes of white, green, and blue – according to the division to which each Druid belongs.

The Brahmins are the highest caste, and form the priesthood in India. Not all Brahmins belong to this caste, but a large group does. In early times, when a Hindu turned fifty, he renounced his home and family – and went to wander in the wilderness. Those of the Druidical religion did much the same thing. In Scotland, a monk often left his monastery and went to live in a cave. Like the Hindus, they led a spiritual life.

In ancient times, the Druids of North Wales were gathered at Mona in Anglesey, where pilgrims came for instruction. Pilgrims in India gathered at Nalonda to study at the University. The Chinese pilgrims came and, what they learned went home – they brought these teachings with them. One

Chinese writer said the school in India was enclosed by a brick wall and there were tiny rooms for each pilgrim to stay in.

The teaching of the philosophers were so widespread in the ancient world that it was thought that Buddha was called Pythagoras by the Greeks. If this is true, then the mystery of the way knowledge spread in the ancient world is solved.

In a cave near Bombay is a statue of the Hindu trinity – Brahma, Vishnu, and Siva.

PROPAGANDA

Propaganda manipulates thought through words and symbols. One of the most famous examples of propaganda occurred with the Babylonians in their creation epic. In early Mesopotamia, the Babylonians' epic of creation, cosmology, and theology was extant throughout Mesopotamia and represents their religious thought for several millennia. It now rests in the British Museum. Instead of representing the orthodox belief of the time, it was heretical.

Large numbers of cuneiform tablets were discovered that depict the creation legend as it really was known. Marduk was posited as the most important god in the heretical version. And it outlined how he gained his status. The actual creation part of the tablet was small, and Marduk loomed large and important. This bit of propaganda, to make Marduk an important god, to be famous and revered was all made up as a god needed a city to revere him, and Marduk was without such an attribute. Nonetheless this cosmology soon became the most popular in the ancient world.

PYRAMID

Egypt is a land of mystery. Its origins are in the very beginning of ancient history. While studying ancient Egypt, one sometimes feels under the thrall of an ancient eye observing the soul at work. The Great Pyramid is at the very center of Egyptian mystery and is associated with the creation of the universe. The mystery of the pyramid is as ancient as civilization – for it was created at its dawning. It's actually a disappointing sight to the tourist, as it's not as large as imagination makes it. That is illusion, because up close it is very large indeed. It's a symbol in its form – the familiar pyramid or triangle.

People who are superstitious think the pyramid is symbolic of black or white magic – while those who study mysteries think it symbolizes Divine Law. The sacred triangle was part of Egyptian belief, but the rectangle had no special significance. The square, however, was made of four triangles and was therefore sacred.

The Great Pyramid was thought of as a tomb by the Egyptians. It was almost impossible to study it and draw correct conclusions about it. Smaller pyramids were tombs, but the Great Pyramid was much more. Because the Nile floods annually, the various pyramids were not built near it, but were generally built to the west. Blowing sands have ruined a great many of the pyramids – they're pock-marked by sandstorms. The smooth face has been eaten away, leaving the building blocks in view. The reason the pyramid form was chosen over a rectangle (other than religious reasons) was to keep the damage from sandstorms at a minimum.

The Great Pyramid was at one time surrounded by a plaza. From above, the walls of the plaza are still visible. The structure of the plaza helped to keep sandstorms at bay.

The interior of the Great Pyramid wasn't seen until 820 A.D. The mystery schools that exist in Egypt say that the interior was used for initiation rituals. The tunnels open into chambers for initiates at various levels of progress. The highest chamber was the king's chamber. There's a connection between the Sphinx and the Great Pyramid: A discovery was made of a secret court, or temple, between the paws and breast of the Sphinx.

There was a concerted effort on the part of the secret schools to keep knowledge of the Great Pyramid's secret chambers from the public, and the falsehoods they used are still used today. There is a curse, they say, on those who reveal to the uninitiated the existence of the chambers and tunnels, as if it is fact that the Great Pyramid was a temple of mystical instruction and ritual. Even tourists who have visited the chambers are warned to say there's nothing inside, or the curse will get them. Thus, many returning tourists keep the secret still.

The king's chamber is defaced with the names of visitors on the walls. Sections of the decor of the chambers and most art objects have been stored in secret museums, and only the initiated may see them.

The Great Pyramid is a building of wisdom and prophets, and its symbols are mysteries for all generations to decipher. The ancients were concerned with these matters – even as they made the Rosetta Stone to help clarify the meaning of their hierogliphics.

In case the Rosetta Stone was lost, the ancients decided to use symbology to explain the Great Pyramid. Geometry, math, and cosmology were chosen in combination to form a decipherable language.

The site of the Great Pyramid was chosen for the future generations to understand. The ancients knew the amount of land that makes up Earth – and the relationship of the point in the surface to the main stars in the heavens. If future generations interpreted these symbols correctly, then they could interpret the rest of the symbols making up the Pyramid. There is symbology in the mysterious dimensions of the interior of the Pyramid. By interpreting them correctly, the symbols represent the future of the world in its prophecies. Other pyramids are oriented to astrological alignment, but the Great Pyramid is more than that. Stonehenge is the other monument to the mysteries of prophecy.

The Great Pyramid was erected about a thousand years before Stonehenge by people known as the Aryan-Phoenicians. The measurements of the Great Pyramid, located in the exact land center of the Earth, reveals the Egyptian knowledge of astronomy and geometry. After careful measurement of all aspects of the Great Pyramid, researchers found that there is great genius in the way it was put together.

The word *Pyramid* is Greek, not Egyptian. This in itself is symbolic. It means *fire, light,* and *measure.* The Greeks took the word from the Phoenician (light-measure). There is a similar word in Hebrew too. The Pyramid symbolizes revelations through measurements. The unit of measurement used to build the Pyramid is its own unique size – and doesn't correspond to an American inch.

Using the Pyramid unit of measurements, its size and dimensions reveal the story of past centuries before the Pyramid was even built – the story of times when it was being built, and for the centuries to come in prophecy. The Pyramid was far from just being a tomb. It's a symbol of all knowledge of ancient and modern times.

One of the prophecies revealed in the Great Pyramid has to do with the Great Flood as well as other prophecies, such as important wars between nations and the development of religions. The Exodus of the Israelites from Egypt was foretold. The birth of Christ was another prophecy revealed. There is a pyramid measurement that prophecies His crucifixion as well.

The Great pyramid at Giza about which I speak was begun about 2900 B.C. The cement that was used to build it was as fine as a sheet of paper, and was much stronger than modern cement. The pyramid was built in perfect proportion. The top of the Pyramid was at the exact center of the bottom. A slit in the top of the Pyramid was used for astronomical sighting and was directed at Polaris.

Today, some would say that advanced aliens helped construct the Pyramid and the Sphinx, and that they may have come from Polaris. Someday we will know for certain.

Q R

Queen
Quadriga

Raven
Rebirth
Red
Renaissance Painters
Rigveda
Rose

QUEEN

The Queen has always symbolized the feminine principle or the mother. In history she is rarely portrayed alone. She is usually in the company of a king. This situation is typical of Western society where the role of women has always been secondary to that of men.

In fairytales and legends, however, there is much made of queens (Spenser's "The Faerie Queene"). They're portrayed positively as well as negatively as important witches. The situation indicates the higher role of women in ancient society before the Judeo-Christian culture took over.

QUADRIGA

The Quadriga is a symbol of space and time in the universe. It's a variant of the square and carries the same symbolism associated with the number four. It's a symbol of four horses drawing a chariot and an intersection of the Circles of Heaven with Earth, making manifest the world. In some interpretations, the four horses represent the four elements.

RAVEN

The raven went to battle with many of the ancient heroes. It ate dead flesh and was the pet of the Norse god Odin. It soared in victory and looked crestfallen when there was a defeat.

Two ravens sat on Odin's shoulders. One he called Mind and the other Memory. They whispered advice to him.

In some legends the raven was said to be a white bird. In the story of Noah and the Ark, this was the bird Noah sent out to look for land – a white raven. In Jewish mythology, the raven was the symbol of Satan.

In ancient times, especially in Greece and Rome, the raven had the characteristics of the god Saturn, who was the bearer of evil tidings. The day that Cicero was murdered, a raven came to his room and croaked long and loud.

But in different cultures, the raven was associated with cosmic powers. Its coins were associated with farmland instead of death. So to the Indians of North America, the raven was thought to be the creator of the visible world that we know.

One old hero had a raven who was a prophet. When he lay dying, he asked that his head be buried on Lincoln hillside in London. The raven followed the funeral procession to the site, and now ravens can be seen protecting the Tower of London where the crown jewels lie in state.

REBIRTH

There is no knowledge of when the idea of rebirth had its origin. Forty centuries ago the Indians believed in rebirth, and it may have traveled there from Chaldea.

In an Egyptian papyrus from 300 B.C. there appears the question and answer "Who is the author of rebirth? The Son of God." The same papyrus states that no one can be saved without rebirth, and that the material body should not be confused with the spiritual body. To be reborn, one must conquer excesses of the body and its senses and develop willpower. When this is done and the rebel in us is conquered, Divinity comes into being. This holy thought of rebirth was supposed to be recited outdoors facing southwest at the time of sunset and toward the east at sunrise. The doctrine was supposed to be kept secret. I can imagine the esoteric flak that would have befallen the practitioners if their prayers were found out by the higher-ups!

The Egyptian papyrus said that when man sees a sincere vision brought to birth by God's mercy, he will pass into a new body that will never die and is now born of the Mind. Mary Baker Eddy must have studied this concept to form the Christian Science Church – which believes all is from Mind, or God. The state of being of mind brings peace and joy.

This goal of rebirth was the foundation of mysticism. It means that one returns to a world governed by the spirit of wisdom and love, and where the animal in man obeys the spirit.

The serpent coiled in the cross was a symbol of regeneration, because the snake shed its skin and is born again. The trefoil is a symbol of the Trinity.

RED

Red is the most popular of colors. The color red symbolizes love – falling in love and even God's love of mankind. Think of red roses and Valentines' boxes of candy – all red.

Red can stand for rebellious, for blood and battle, for victory. The Vikings showed a red shield when they were about to attack, as did the modern Danish navy. Primitive tribesmen, and even early Romans, painted their bodies with red pigment before going into battle, finding the color red a source of energy.

Red is the color of Mars, the Roman god of war and bloodshed. The planet Mars is often referred to as "the red planet," due to its reddish glow in the night sky.

Because red can be easily seen, ambulances and fire engines are painted red. The color can signal danger, too, and is used for stop signs and stop lights.

Red symbolizes Christ's passion in the Church and sometimes represents the Holy Ghost.

RENAISSANCE PAINTERS

In the Renaissance, some symbols were meant to represent the names of the people who ordered the artwork that adorned their homes. Sometimes benefactors asked the painters to do a loggia, or some other unimportant piece of their home, and they'd let their imaginations run wild. The images would be funny and the symbols full of wit and gaiety – none of the decoration such as one would find in the paintings adorning the important rooms of the house.

The paintings Botticelli did of Venus and other gods and goddesses came to his canvas at the time religious art was important. Mythological themes were found on such objects as caskets but rarely, if ever, in large paintings. His work was a novelty in the 1470s. *Primavera* was the first of Botticelli's mythologies. This was painted during a period when a pagan revival was taking place and is associated with the Florentine, Lorenzo de Medici. *The Birth of Venus* and the *Primavera* originally were in the home of Lorenzo di Pierfrancesco, a cousin of Lorenzo de Medici. *Primavera* was commissioned for his new villa, Villa di Castello. Venus stood for Humanitas. The young owner of the villa was instructed by the painting to have virtue and gentleness of spirit.

The question surrounding *Venus* and *Primavera* is: Are they painting diagrams of symbolism, or are they just pictures of gods for the purpose of form and influence? In any case, they are more than just decorations. The myth contains the meaning and therefore the power.

RIGVEDA

Cosmic language is found in objects and the alphabet. Meaning must be found in them. Visible objects have mystical meaning. The symbol is the language. Symbols are selected over words as the expression of living meaning. Symbols overcome racial and ethnic embodiments of living meaning, and the mind is that which finds the meanings.

The reason the seers and others speak mystically is because the gods love mysticism. The cow in India is sacred because she symbolizes motherhood. The richness of meanings in the Vedic texts lend to symbolism a welcome authority.

Bhutos, or material objects, are idealized and made symbols. A tree became a Tree of Life, the jar a holder of unlimited existence. Unraveling Vedic symbols is like unweaving cloth. It's complex, and everything relates to everything else.

Agni is the supreme god in Rigveda. It is an immortal principle among mortal man, the spirit of materialization, or matter made living. Aditi is the mother and Daksha the son. The principle of Energy is divided into Matter, Life, and Mind. These are the three births of Agni.

When the seed which has the child in it opens, the child immediately wants food. This is the story of life and a feature of life. When Agni is without food, it becomes fire and burns up the body. Food, *soma*, must always exist to keep the children of life serene.

There is a creative principle, Narayana Purusha, who sleeps in the ocean's womb. The ocean is both pure water and milk from the cow. This is symbolized by mixing *soma* and milk in a vessel. The two principles, Agni and *soma*, mix and form seeds of life. Because butter globules in milk activate its nutrious force, it is the form of fire in sacrifice. It's taken as the fertilizing seed. This symbol is known as Chria. Universal nature is represented by the universal cow. The universe is her milk and the life principle is the butter in the milk. This is called Purishad Ajya in Rigveda. The sun is the calf of this universal cow, and also represents the bull in that its rays enliven nature. The rays are the fertilizing seed. The sun's responsibility is Fire and Water or Heat and Cold.

ROSE

The rose is a very old and complex symbol, and appears often in literature, especially in the work of T. S. Eliot, James Joyce, and William Butler Yeats.

It can be a symbol of love, beauty, or attitudes and beliefs. Some writers have used the rose to symbolize the values of our ancestors. In the *Divine Comedy*, Dante used a rose to symbolize the Virgin, Paradise, and Divine Love.

Religious and romantic writers use the rose to express an intangible idea.

Symbols flourished most in the Middle Ages, and in the romantic works of the nineteenth and twentieth centuries. In the twentieth century, rose symbols and other images have come to mean the loss of faith and sometimes emotional confusion.

In the nineteenth century the rose sometimes symbolized subjective values to the sensitive soul.

The rose has symbolized love and women, and the religious divine love and fertility. Christ and the Virgin are associated with the rose. The flower also depicts motherhood and mother nature. It has also symbolized the mother country and is in the heraldry of England and Ireland. Also close to motherhood, the rose symbolizes birth and rebirth.

The rose has also symbolized sorrow. It dies soon after it blooms, and is thorny. The thorns bring pain to mind. The blood of martyrs is symbolized by the rose. Enjoy the rose before it withers!

The rose symbolizes the happiest dreams of mankind. Some think the rose looks like the female sexual organs, and Freud considered it a sexual symbol.

The rose was used in aphrodisiacs composed by witches. And there are many mentions in folklore of the rose signifying love and marriage. Songs of early times made mention of the rose – and fairytales abound with the rose – *Snow White and Rose Red* pops quickly to mind.

The early appearance of the rose in spring makes it part of ceremonies dedicated to spring.

Jung believed that there must be a balance between the conscious and unconscious mind, and that death and resurrection are part of all religions. There are parallels among these religions and the rose with its perfect shape, and its birth and rebirth in beauty account for its eminence. It's part of Jung's mandala, a symbol in dreams and myths which constitute its circular center. As a mandala the rose symbolizes rebirth, psychic harmony, and fulfillment of being.

The rose of the Egyptian goddess Isis had material and solar meanings. Isis was wife of the sun god Osiris and mother of Horus, who became the sun god after Osiris was murdered. Isis was mother of all living things – the rose represented the female generative organs.

The religion of Isis reached into Greek and Roman theology. And the Virgin Mary is depicted as a rose symbol. Aphrodite (or Venus) is associated with the rose. Venus was in charge of mortal love. Like Isis, she was considered an earth mother.

One legend of Aphrodite had the rose bloom at her birth from the sea. Her symbolic rose appeared in marriages and other customs celebrating love.

Eros, Aphrodite's son, used roses as did the Three Graces. Dionysus, god of the trees, used the rose at orgies to symbolize the life force.

Newlyweds slept on rose petals thrown on their beds, and pillows were filled with petals.

S

SCALES

The Egyptian Book of the Dead speaks of
a weighing of the soul as part of the tests
after death. The soul is weighed for its
deeds.

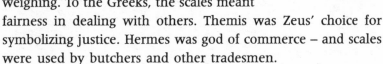

In Greek mythology, Zeus owned
the scales and let Hermes do the soul
weighing. To the Greeks, the scales meant
fairness in dealing with others. Themis was Zeus' choice for
symbolizing justice. Hermes was god of commerce – and scales
were used by butchers and other tradesmen.

In the West scales symbolize equality and justice.

SECOND COMING

While waiting for Christ to appear again, the anticipated reign
of God on this wicked earth was expressed, in early times, by
a cross surmounted by a sphere. This symbol has been found
as far back as 1301 B.C. Gradually, over the centuries, other
symbols were added and indicate a living tradition. The Orb of
Power in the British Isles may symbolize the reign of God, as
well as more earthly royalty.

A symbol of the globe with crosses covering it came to
mean the universal spread of Christianity. On another orb, the
initials IC indicating Christ and the longing for His return are
indicated by a heart and a fleur-de-lis.

The Kingdom of Heaven was often symbolized by a crescent inside a circle.

The Holy Hills are sometimes associated with the globe
and cross of the Second Coming. These hills emblemize the
prophecy that the House of the Lord would be found in the
mountains. People of the earth will trek to the Holy Place. God
will, at this time, judge and rebuke people and they shall beat
their swords into plowshares and their spears into pruning
hooks. All people will walk in the name of the Lord forever
and ever. And the Lord shall reign for evermore from Mount
Zion. A symbol of these times is a man carrying the scales of

justice and the Sword of the Spirit, and he's crowned with a trefoil. Another figure bears the cross and globe.

The *Lux* cross has the letter *R* within a circle and was the symbol of the City of Regeneration. On it were the initials IR, which stood for Jesus Redemptor.

The numbers of Millennium or Second Coming symbols indicate how many people held the belief of the imminence of the Second Coming. Here we are again at a Millennium (the year 2000), and we're surrounded with the ideas of the weather causing floods and earthquakes and volcanic eruptions – which all mean the Second Coming is near – for those who believe in such signs.

SEVEN
Seven turns up like four and three – in almost all parts of our lives. There is seventh heaven, and a broken mirror means seven years' bad luck. There are the seven dwarfs from Disney (and fairytales). *The Seventh Veil* is a book. There are seven seas, seven colors in the spectrum of color, seven planets, and seven notes in one scale of music.

Rome was arranged on seven hills, and there were seven wonders of the world. Pythagoras considered seven to be the ideal number. In the East, as well as the West, seven heavens are described. There are Seven Deadly Sins. There are seven days in the week . . . it goes on and on. Obviously the number seven is important now and in the past, and shall be in the future.

SEX
The worship of Pan in Greece brought about some indecent practices. Kehm was worshipped in Egypt. Khem's symbol was a gnat. The Egyptians worshipped the sex organ. The temple of Karnac showed men in paintings with their phalluses erect. So it, too, was associated with sex worship.

Captain James Cook found sexually-related religious ceremonies in the South Pacific. An observed ceremony included a young man and woman engaged in the sex act before the group of worshippers.

India had similar worship. An Indian woman of a certain caste was chosen. Rites followed, and a circle was purified with wine. The sex act was consummated, and took place before an altar. These sex-worship incidents may be found in ancient Egypt, Greece, Rome, India, China, and Japan, and also in Peru. Sex worship, therefore, was found in primitive religions of early man.

Sacred prostitution in Babylonia, Ninevah, Corinth, and India took place in temples there. The money earned from prostitution went for repair and upkeep of the temple. The children born of these unions formed a separate, superior class.

In India, a temple prostitute was called "Woman of the Idol." As many as a thousand prostitutes lived in the temples of Eryx and Corinth.

With civilization, worshipping sex was no longer as open as in the primitive cultures. Symbolism began to play a part. Priests initiated in the darker rituals became the norm. Sex was still worshipped, but covertly. Sex symbols may still be found in today's Egypt, Greece, India, China, and Japan.

One kind of symbolism had to do with the deified object. Upright objects represented the penis. This symbolism predates Freud's phallic symbol, and he probably came to his conclusions about it by studying ancient religions.

Some qualities of animals were also symbols. The bull, because of his great strength and protean sexual power, was symbolic of sex. Fish – including the dolphin – symbolized the female.

Fire is the male symbol, and water the female. Thus Venus came from the sea. Fire was usually found in sun worship. The sun is symbolic of the male – it stands for the phallic power of nature. The god Hermes, who was the God of Fecundity, is at times portrayed in phallic glory.

Another type of symbolism grew up in India. Extra arms and legs were attached to the deity – even more than one head. This was in order to demonstrate a number of qualities. The god was shown with benevolent and violent faces – so he was both a generator and destroyer. Another deity was androgynous.

The obelisk was an early phallic symbol. Sun worship revolved around the obelisk. Chinese pagodas are part of phallic symbolism. Indeed, the spires of modern churches are thought to be phallic in origin, imitating the obelisk.

Stonehenge is thought to show phallic symbolism. The simple Maypole is also phallic and is associated with worship of the male member in ancient times.

With the passing of time, some old symbols took on hidden meaning. The symbols for male and female were hidden in such objects as a menhir, a pyramid, and a trident for male attributes – and a crescent moon, darkness, and the cup took on female meanings. Together, they symbolized the source of life.

Some scholars identify fire worship with sex worship. The Rosicrucians use symbolism to express religious thought. The male generative emblem is the First Principle.

Sex worship continues in India today. In the caves of elephants near Bombay, there is a phallus which is sprinkled with water during ceremonies. And the female sculptures have huge breasts. It is not considered bad form to worship at the caves.

In a temple in Japan, a large upright stone is worshipped, especially by women. They leave offerings there – small wooden phalluses.

The early people of the Near East believed in sun and moon worship, as well as allegories portraying the seasons and, therefore, the fertile and infertile periods of nature. These were expressed in a philosophy which made the entire universe part of a sexual system. The earth, with her womb, was the mother – and the father was the sun who impregnated her with light and heat. The Sun God was thought to be the father of all existence.

All the sun and moon cults in these early times were fertility cults, and the difference between sun and sex worship was one of emphasis. The Hindus still believe in a mother and father god and goddess. The earth goddess is Prthivi and Dysus is the sky-god.

As far as the symbols of the sun and moon deities go, painters portrayed the new spring sun as a chubby baby, and the winter as an old man.

Everything on earth or in the sky was made male or female, according to positive and negative aspects. For example, male attributes were positive – summer, fire, square, etc. – and female attributes were negative – earth, death, evil, and round.

By these associations, wells, lakes, valleys, and caves, were places of the gods and of special veneration.

Holes in the earth from which vapors rose, or hot springs, were designated oracles. Delphi was in that kind of place.

Mountains, or domelike structures were figured to be breasts of nature. Sacred altars were erected there. Mounds and pyramids that are naturally formed are esteemed too, and are found all over the earth.

The temples of the Babylonians were built on mounds and called mountains of the world.

In Palestine, since the times of Abraham, the sacred temple altars were built on hills or high places.

The early Chaldeans believed the world was formed like a human figure, in which Egypt was the heart.

In Jerusalem, at the Church of the Holy Sepulchre, is the most important part of the Church. It is the nave east of the rotunda. There is a short column there that is a symbol of the Tree of Life, and marks the center of the world (as the ancients knew it).

The old Irish believed that the center of the world was at the boundaries of Meath, where five provinces meet. The Archdruids put a large stone there that is the "stone of the parts."

The Chinese visualized the earth as being square, and the sky round. China's sacred temple of the moon is round to match the sky. This belief is carried through to the Chinese coin, which is round and has a small square in the center of it. The symbolism of the square and the circle represented, to the Chinese, the divine source of all things.

The male sex organ took on a three-part image and, in combination with the female symbol, a four-part symbol came to represent the foundations of the earth. The three-part male god seems to have been the origin of the Christian Trinity.

In the Assyrian Triad, there was Asshut, Ance, and Ea. Asshut was a symbol of fortune and happiness. He was the upright, or male organ, representation of the Triad. The triad was a threefold sex symbol. The right testicle represented Ance (fire, light) and the left testicle was Ea (for water). Betis was the female goddess of the four-part god. They all represented the perfect earth.

The cross appeared wherever there was worship of fertility and sex. Its intersecting arms represented the sun's rays, and was imbued with life-giving power.

The Orientals divide all objects into male and female. They are classified by function. A hoe and plow is male, as it opens the earth for the seed. At Indian wedding ceremonies, a plow is sometimes set up under a canopy to symbolize fertility.

Priests sometimes wore female gowns, and priestesses wore male robes. The custom has persisted in the Catholic and Episcopal churches to the present. They represent the unity of the sexes. The interdependence of male and female is thoroughly Oriental in this philosophy.

In India, where many ancient symbols persist, a red line is painted on the forehead of a boychild in the Parsee ceremony, and a round mark is put on the girlchild. The straight line represents the rays of the sun that fertilize, and the round mark represents the earth, which is fertilized.

Modern followers of Vishnu, among the Hindus, mark their foreheads with a white, U-shaped symbol in the center of which is painted a red line. This again is the symbol of male-female fertility.

SICKLE

Cronus, the Greek God of time and agriculture is always shown with a sickle. Saturn, the Roman equivalent of Cronus, was also known as the god of agriculture and bore a sickle. In Europe later on, the sickle turned into a scythe, as agricultural implements grew in number. The scythe is also a symbol of Saturn. Tempus, Father Time, carried a scythe and an hourglass as his symbols.

The scythe became associated with death as a symbol of advancing time. From the fourteenth century until today, death has been depicted as a skeleton. The scythe came to be his attribute and his name, the Grim Reaper. Meanwhile, the scythe kept its original meaning of the harvest and hope – in raising fine crops.

SILVER AND GOLD

Silver, as the color white, indicates the symbol of purity and chastity. The term "silver-tongued" is commonly applied to Sunday mornings television preachers.

Silver is a moon metal associated with occult practices, as well as being symbolic of darkness and the unconscious mind. It opposes gold, which reflects the sun and is representative of life and light.

In the Tarot, the concept is expressed by the fourteenth card in the deck, which is Temperance. It is also known as the angel of time and shows a figure pouring liquid from a silver into a gold cup. If silver is the moon, and gold the sun, and the liquid is the spirit, then the conscious and unconscious mind are combined to be an invincible power.

Silver, with its occult connection to the moon, is a perfect metal for the making of amulets and talismans. Mohammed forbade the use of any other metal for the making of these objects.

One eighteenth-century book suggests that a talisman engraved on silver, when the moon is astrologically well-placed, would make one not only rich and honored, but happy as well.

Gold, because it is valuable and the color of the sun, is close to the mystic aspect of the sun. It is symbolic of purity and divinity, holiness, and goodness – and this explains why it is often found in church vestments and cups, etc.

Anything golden or made of gold has this quality of perfection. Gold is often condemned in the Bible because of its association to worldly wealth – but that doesn't stop the church from using it.

Gold is sometimes a symbol of idolatry and greed. Witness King Midas who turned everything he touched into gold, and also the legend of Aaron and the Israelites who worshipped the golden calf.

Gold can also be a symbol of spiritual treasures – as in the myths and sagas of those who seek hidden treasure.

The fabled elixir of life was associated with gold. Paracelsus, the fabled sixteenth-century occultist, is said to have actually made the elixir of life from gold. In its liquid form, it was thought to be good for heart trouble, especially as the heart is ruled by the sun.

SKULL

In modern times the skull is a symbol for poison in all languages. In pirate days crossed bones usually accompanied the skull, which symbolized fear and absolute danger.

The Nazis chose a skull to decorate the SS caps.

The skull was an element in church vestments and in the coats of arms of religious families. But the skull often symbolizes death and corruption of the flesh. Among the most famous skulls in literature was Shakespeare's Yorick.

SNAKES
In the Babylonian culture, evil brought forth serpents which were poisonous and had sharp teeth. They took other forms, too, fishlike men, or dragons, or mad dogs. Merodach was the good spirit who sought them.

Apollo – the God of Day to the Greeks – struggled with and killed a python.

Christ promised his disciples the power to crush serpents and scorpions with their feet.

Isaiah prophesied that at the Second Coming, Christ would strike down Leviathan – the great serpent – and kill him for all time.

The human fear of snakes is demonstrated in stories in which snakes were killed by God or gods.

SPHINX
The Sphinx symbolizes mystery, inscrutability, and divinity. It also stands for the bad characteristics of women, such

as cruelty and erotic obsession. Herodotus named the Egyptian Sphinx after the Greek oracle that asked each passerby a riddle and strangled him if he didn't know the correct answer.

STAIRS

Stairs do the same thing as doorways – moving from one state of mind to another.

Winding stairways represent movement that is mysterious. Spiral stairs move towards the sun.

STAR

Stars represent hope and good fortune. The stars on the American flag symbolize the number of states and stand for freedom from the colonial world and the past.

The Symbol of Health – which is a five-pointed star – was the Seal of Solomon, with which he worked miracles of marvelous proportion. He worked magic with this talisman and kept evil genies at bay.

STONE WORSHIP

Stones sometimes symbolize God and were often worshipped in the past.

Moses spoke of a rock as the father of the Israelites. And there is a psalm that speaks of God as a rock.

The Kafirs in India worship rocks because they don't know the image of God.

The Maoris of New Zealand put rocks in the ground in a circle to represent their gods.

In Brittany the menhirs represented God. The Arabs worshipped an ancient stone known as Manah.

In many languages, stones take on the meaning of the Fire of Life.

White pebbles called "god stones" were put in Irish graves.

One of the largest monoliths to be found in England is at Drizzlecombe in Devonshire. *Drizzle* means Enduring Light God and *combe* means hillside or hollow.

Stone monoliths are also known as Amberics. St. Ambrose's name derives from Amberic. One of the many names of the Celtic Jupiter was Ambrose. Stonehenge is in the village of Ambresbury.

The Greeks symbolized Mercury, Apollo, Neptune, and Hercules with a square stone. Venus was worshipped as a white pyramid by the Paphians, and Bacchus as a pillar.

A cone-shaped stone was the symbol of Bel, and the Romans worshipped the sun as a black cone.

The infinite God was worshipped in Cornwall as a stone orb, sometimes painted gold. The Celtic clechebrath was an enormous orb balanced so carefully that it vibrated when touched.

On the island of Skye, in a small chapel dedicated to St. Columba, is a small blue stone on the altar. The stone is bathed in sea water by fisherman desiring a safe trip and a good catch.

STORKS

Storks symbolize taking care of the elderly in Europe, and they also signify parental love.

The stork symbolizes fertility and piousness and in classic times was associated with Juno and Ceres, the goddesses of marriage.

Storks eat snakes and so symbolize a watchdog over evil.

The stork is known as the bringer of babies; and in Germany the stork is therefore considered the bird of good luck.

SUN

All of Earth depends on the sun for light, heat, and fertility. It has been worshipped by nearly every culture and country and religion. Among the sun gods are Apollo and the Persian deity, Mithras. Our holy day of the sun is Sunday. The old Testament even regards the Lord as the sun. The sun is a sign of divinity and a healer. The sun can be an enemy too – with drought and death.

The flag of Japan bears a sun.

Gods are sometimes portrayed with sun rays emanating from their heads; witness the halos of the saints and the king's crowns. Sometimes poets and philosophers have halos. Homer and Virgil have been depicted with halos as, of course, have Christ and the Holy Family. In statuary, the halo was sometimes bejeweled.

To some kings, the sun symbol meant they were equal to God. King Louis XIV of France was known as the Sun King.

The sun is a symbol of freedom and beginnings. Some Spanish speaking countries in South America chose the sun for their flags after breaking away from Spain. Even the Soviets chose the sun as an early symbol in 1917.

Incas in Peru claim they are descended from the sun and the moon, and among some South American tribes the sun is a man and the moon is his wife.

Because rising and setting of the sun can be calculated to the nearest second, it's a symbol of reliability. A great many churches and cathedrals in a variety of religions (Christianity included) face the East and the Rising Sun.

In all the world, the East was the direction that signified life, light, and birth. The West and Southwest were the directions of death. Temples, cathedrals, and churches were oriented to the East at the time of the vernal equinox, or the sunrise point, on the day sacred to the saint for whom the church was named.

In England, a great many of the churches are built so that the sun shines through the window above the altar. Worshippers, then, face the sun. Churches and cathedrals oriented to the vernal equinox are, among others, Westminster Abbey in London, Notre Dame in Paris, and St. Peter's in Rome.

In the Orient, the dead are buried so as to catch the rising sun. In Europe, the practice took hold too.

Among the Babylonians, North was the direction symbolizing heaven. The Jews felt the North was the sacred place of the Lord.

Sun worship prevails in dealing cards counter-clockwise, or to the sun, and also performing dance movements thusly.

SWASTIKA

Besides the Christian cross, the other great and widely-known cross is the Swastika. When the arms point to the left, it is a female symbol. Thus, because it's female, it's an unlucky sym- bol in ancient interpretation. When the arms point to the right, the luck is good. It represents health and happiness. The Hindus believe that it frightens away evil.

To the Buddhists in the Orient, the swastika symbolized "the thousand truths" of Buddah. It's placed on statuary and other images of Buddah.

From the dawn of civilization, the swastika was the symbol of life. It was carved on idols and is, perhaps, the oldest symbol of man.

SYMBOLIST POETS

Mallarmé

A French poet who decorated his art with jewels and baubles, Stephane Mallarmé symbolized his poetry with glances through mirrors, and the golden monster of his famous work symbolized poetry itself. He wrote of dragons, a symbol of death, and of fauna and other mythical beasts. In his work is emotion, pain, and desire. He worked to write the quintessential poem. His images, by alchemy, were changed to grander meanings and he suffered over his poems, expanding his intellectual capacities to encompass their levels of symbolism with proper words. He had the trimorpha vision – suffering, passion, death – that was the history of Christ.

Mallarmé believed that beauty was a lie in the face of the cosmos and space. But a lie was better than nothing. He believed that death was the truth, and beauty the lie we use to cover up the truth of death. He had this view for thirty years. In one poem he describes his philosophy in full – "Las Noces d'erodiade." In this he expands his concept of beauty. The golden monster – beauty – fights the monster of the void but finds itself over the void, with the written word.

Grief, Mallarmé thought, denies the void beyond. Art is antidestiny. Another poem, "Toast funébre" portrays this conflict of beauty and emptiness. Memory, he believes, fights the void. The beautiful denies death. But memory is your own, and your only weapon against the void.

Mallarmé wrote as an act of faith in the face of despair. He believed that one's dreams are in conflict with one's destiny. And the whole of poetry should be about this. He became obsessed with the philosophical concept of the conflict of dreams and reality. He rejected Christianity and so turned, with unhappiness, to his philosophy. He believed out of death came the essence of life and events. The Golden Monster was the void of death. He was a seventeenth-century poet who was daring and hoping that he was correct in his philosophy.

VERLAINE

Verlaine had a bit of the countryside in his work – not at all a city-bred poet. He was childlike, and these qualities are the key to understanding Paul Verlaine. In French, he was a näif. He was not always sincere – and scorned other poets (though he was a great friend of Mallarmé and they respected each other). He disparaged those who were emotional in their work. He did not suffer fools gladly. This näiveté, which he referenced so often, was also applied to his love of children. He wrote of children "Gosses," and applied his childlike quality. He speaks of the näiveté of his childhood too, and his lack of guile. He feels he was unchanged by his years and remained childlike. He did recognize the complexities of adulthood, however. He wanted to regain his childhood by the act of writing and rediscovered it there.

Another aspect of Verlaine's näiveté is his sensuality. He wrote poetry that expressed this, and it is one of the aspects of his work. He also described landscapes with this same sensuality. Farmhouses become female. He never thinks of the farmers as rough, rugged men of the land; he thinks of them as näifs, jolly and good-natured. He uses the symbolism of the näif to describe priests of the church and the holy pictures in the church. If he liked a piece of artwork, wherever it was to be found, he applauded it in terms of his näif philosophy. He longed to be free of intellectual dogma.

One aspect of Verlaine to consider is that beneath this shell of näiveté lay an important artist. He hid his art behind the näif philosophy. His work, however, was of the day; people responded to him and his art. These were people of the 1890s and they liked the portrayal of themselves as näifs. Verlaine died in 1896, leaving behind a legacy for a generation of writers to come. They copied his style. After 1918 the worshipfulness disappeared. New poets took his place. Rimbaud and Lautreamont became the new fair-haired poets.

Verlaine made something of a comeback in the 1950s. He had been bruised by critics in the years prior to the fifties. Some sympathetic biographies were written, though not all of his work was brought from oblivion. Apparently, in 1873, Verlaine underwent a conversion to Catholicism, and his critics said it ruined his work. He was great early, and not so poetic later on in his life.

One of Verlaine's mysteries is in the poetic words "*l'espoir luit*" in the poem "Sagesse." No one, it seems, can find the poetic meaning of the words. Much interpretation has taken place, but no one knows what he meant by the poem.

One must know that Verlaine was incarcerated for some time at Le Mons prison. The *"l'espoir luit"* fragment may refer to this time. It seems to have been a draft for a much larger sequence of poems.

Attracted to the painting of the eighteenth century, Verlaine was also taken by the work of Rembrandt. He was an admirer, not a scholar, of the work. He wrote of Rembrandt and spoke of him as a ghost from another time. His work in Holland captures his feeling for Rembrandt.

Mysticism and *gentleness* are words to depict Verlaine's work, and he was a widely read poet from whom references to earlier works were common. He admired the work of Marceline Desbordes-Valmore, and found her poems to be sophisitcated in style. Some of them seemed akin to his own work. He also loved the work of Baudelaire and his *"fleur de mai"* was a schoolboy's ideal.

RIMBAUD

Arthur Rimbaud is the penultimate symbolist poet. Many critics wrote about him in the forties and fifties. Rimbaud believed in love – that it was the great force for resolving disputes. He used the structure of his poetry to tame chaos. He chose the symmetry of the preacher's sermon to name the poem "Genie." Thus he was a theoretician among other styles. He also wrote of the seasons as conquering man. He wrote of sexuality in the Genie, and balanced love and rhetoric. He uses the Gospel of redemption. He writes of these visions in adoration though he negates superstition. He doesn't believe in the Second Coming of God, but that He is already here with us. He takes us to the center of the images he erects, then expounds that reality is illusionary. He may have been among the first poets to announce that the traditional God is dead. He gives one hope in his philosophy that God is here with us. He believes there are those who will find a new vision. The fertility of the mind matches the fertility of the universe. Salvation, he believes, is here and now. He is almost a modern-day Christian Scientist in his beliefs about God. He is splendid. With his poems he heals the pains of life – he does not just pour out his philosophy. He rounds it out in the mode of rhetoric and therefore creates poems of great beauty. Rimbaud is magical and comes to the muse via the subconscious. He doesn't write of daily occurrences, but the mysticism of the life that is around us – almost from a dream.

Rimbaud's themes for his poetry were few. He used the idealism of youth as a subject, as well as religious subjects. He worked for the dramatic instead of the mundane, and this bent brought forth the symbolism he chose. His poetry was to become patterned and free of the common sense of words. He strove for impression rather than representational images during the 1870s.

CLAUDEL

Paul Claudel wrote extensively to his contemporary, Paul Valery, and both were part of Mallarmé's circle of friends. Claudel traveled in China and Valery wrote him there. Claudel was a definite Catholic, while Valery was a nonbeliever. Both poets traveled extensively.

When reading his poetry, Claudel wished his readers to search for the deeper meaning of his poems. Nothing was simple – the meanings were always intellectually challenging. Claudel saw Titian's works in Madrid. He was influenced by the voluptuous coloring and subjects and reflected the style of Titian in several poems of the period. The reason Claudel and Valery are thought of and studied together is that they copied each other's experiences. If Claudel studied Titian, then Valery studied Rembrandt. Claudel doesn't fall for the mysterious. He works for openness, his words free.

VALERY

Paul Valery wrote about World War I. His career lasted about fifty years. He tried to make his language brilliant – free of vagueness. Linguistics were important to him. He believed in the precision of math. He studied math to gain the texture of his writing. He preferred to describe his subject, not just explain it. Exactness was his goal. Poetry was geometrical to him, and he wrote precisely. The symbols he used most were the sap, the tree, and crystal stones. With knowledge, he hoped to go beyond the physical world. He wrote of the ouroboros (the snake that devours its tail). He wrote much on the theme of love and how love devours. He believed that Eden lay in the mind. His poems brought an acute mental activity. He feels thought, and his brain, growing. Many of his metaphors and symbols were religious. He sought an individual language with which to write each poem.

APOLLINAIRE

Guillaume Apollinaire was a true symbolist, though he was not in the circle of Mallarmé, Claudel, and Valery. He sought expression that was vivid and new, and had an interest in the site (painting, for example). He wrote art criticism and was an early proponent of the Cubists. Paintings were the subject of some of his poems, and he wrote poem-drawings he called *calligrammes*. He made sketches as he wrote his poems on paper. He didn't have musical ability and didn't care for concerts. But music was central to his work. Poetry mimicked the musical thread.

He based some of his poems on folk music and some on hymns. He also used, for rhythm, the poetry of the other symbolists. He would sometimes hum to himself for inspiration. His hymn rhythms are his most insistent. The poetry is read in the stately manner of each hymn. Like the other symbolists, he used little punctuation. This method was meant to lead one into the innermost depths of the poetic line. He sought to find his being in love and poetry. His images are based on song, and we flow with his intention as we read his work. His art works toward the inner sanctum of the soul. One of his themes is that a man's destiny is seen in his love – sometimes unhappy – with its frustrations.

T

TAROT

The Tarot is a foolproof ancient method of fortunetelling. I have used the Tarot for the last thirty years and I've never known it to be wrong. I used to know a man in the CIA, and every time I asked a question of the deck about him, the card indicating "clandestine" would show up. It was simply uncanny.

I've provided here not the fortunetelling meaning of the cards, but their symbolic meaning. To learn the cards, buy a good book on them and memorize them so you can understand the meanings easily. Good luck with your Tarot readings!

GREATER ARCANA

The Magician: He is a sly arbiter of fate – casting the dice and full of tricks. Sometimes he symbolizes unity, sometimes Divine unity. Another interpretation is that the magician represents the will.

The High Priestess: This is the female pope. Some interpretations call her the pope's wife, and others say she symbolizes the mother. She is said to symbolize Divine Law. She represents the secret tradition and the mysteries.

The Empress: She is usually seen full on while the Emperor is seen sideways. She symbolizes universal fecundity and activity in daily life.

The Emperor: The husband of the Empress, he wears the ribbons of chivalry. The Empress and Emperor are a mixture of old and new and the interpretation of the card can involve the old and the new.

The Hierophant (High Priest):   He is symbolized as the spiritual Father and, again, the pope. He has also been interpreted as the Abbot – and the High Priestess as the Abbess – but pope is the more common interpretation. The High Priestess may represent the Church to whom the pope is married – the best symbolic interpretation.

The Lovers: This card has represented marriage since the eighteenth century and is a card of family. The cupid in the card symbolizes love in bloom – not in its fullness but at its beginning when the lovers meet. It symbolizes married faithfulness. The card symbolizes truth, honor, and love, as well as the higher aspects of religious love.

The Chariot: It is pulled by two sphinxes, so it has arcane meanings known in the Egyptian mysteries. In the eighteenth century, the meaning changed and horses were substituted for sphinxes. "The lesser stands for the greater" is the surest meaning of the card. The King in triumph is its outward meaning – kingship won in battle – not inherited. One interpretation says it's a card of Osiris triumphing – the sun conquering in the spring after triumphing over winter.

Fortitude: This card represents one of the main virtues. The female figure is seen closing the mouth of the lion. It symbolizes strength and mastery. The figure represents moral force and all physical and spiritual love.

The Hermit: He is called, besides the Hermit, the Capuchin – or the sage. He symbolizes the search for truth and justice. It's a card more of attainment than quest, however. The light he carries is the light of occult science. And the staff he bears is a magical wand. These symbolic meanings are the same as the fortunetelling meanings. All the roads of the card lead to the heights, and God is at the highest point.

The Wheel of Fortune: The wheel has seven spokes, and the animals ascend and descend. There's a monster with wings on his shoulders, and he wears a crown. It carries two wands in its claws. Symbolically, it is the card of the "wheel of fortune."

Justice: The female figure is supposed to be Astraea, who personified the official Mysteries of the Occult. Justice is one of the three cardinal virtues of the Greater Arcana. The others are Temperance and Fortitude.

The Hanged Man: This card symbolizes prudence and the adept bound by his work. The card shows a man hanging upside down from a gallows to which he is attached by a rope

on one of his ankles. His arms are bound behind him, and one leg crosses the other. He signifies sacrifice in one interpretation.

Death: The card shows the field of life, but there are arms and hands protruding from the ground. One of the heads bears a crown, and a skeleton with a scythe is in the process of cutting it off. The only symbolism of the card is "death." But there are other meanings in change and transformation. It is a card of the death of kings, especially.

Temperance: This is the winged figure of a female – a ministering spirit – who pours liquid between pitchers. There seems little connection to temperance except the pouring of the liquids back and forth, and the symbolic meaning of the card – other than its face value – is shrouded in mystery.

The Devil: In the eighteenth century, this card merely symbolized sexual profligacy. The Devil in the card is naked, has bat wings, and claws for hands and feet. In the right hand is a scepter with a symbol representing fire on it. Two demons are attached by collars to the pedestal on which the Devil stands. One of the demons is male, the other is female. Since 1856 and the judgement of Eliphas Levi, the great occultist, the card has represented a Baphometic figure, which means that it's part goat, and has a torch between its horns. Male and female figures have replaced the demons, but not the symbolism.

The Tower: This card has alternative titles, including God's House and the Tower of Babel. The figures, if the last is the interpretation, are Nimrod (Satan) and his minister falling from the Tower. It's a card representing confusion. If the card symbolizes the House of God, then it means that God has fallen from power and the temple is overthrown.

The Star: This card symbolizes the Dog Star, or Sirius. Grouped about Sirius are seven luminaries, and there is a nude female figure beneath. Her left knee is on the earth, and her right foot on the water. She pours fluid from two vessels. This resembles the symbolism of Revelation.

The Moon: It's a full moon represented on the card set in a heaven full of stars. It's a moon symbolizing increase; it's not waning. She is shedding dew drops from her abundant brightness. There are two towers, and a dog and a wolf baying at her. The card symbolizes the plentitude of the moon.

The Sun: The symbols of the sun are rays and, like the moon, there are drops of dew representing fertility brought by the sun. Court de Gebelin, who interpreted the Tarot, identified the dew drops as the tears of Isis. There is a walled garden on the card (the Garden of Eden) where two naked children play. The sun, in the fortunetelling sense, is a good card and good fortune follows it.

The Last Judgement: Here, an angel sounds his trumpet and the dead arise. Throughout the Greater Arcana of the

Tarot, there is unmistakable symbolism of the Revelation. One interpretation says this card symbolizes evolution, but the card carries none of the signs for this view.

The Fool: Court de Gebelin, the Tarot expert, calls The Fool the zero sum card. Because later interpretations of the cards count them in terms of the Hebrew alphabet, de Gebelin's interpretation has fallen by the wayside – as there is no zero symbol in the Hebrew alphabet. There has been one interpretation that calls it *Shin*, representing two hundred, but this is unsatisfactory.

The Fool is on the edge of a precipice and is holding a wallet. An animal chases him – and he looks over his shoulder unaware he is about to fall. Sometimes he's portrayed as a court jester, and the wallet (in this card) carries vices and follies which the card symbolizes.

The World: The four creatures of the Apocalypse (Revelation again) are grouped around a garland. There is a figure of a woman inside the garland, who wears a scarf. She is dancing and bears a wand in each hand. It is the soul's intoxication with the earth as Paradise. The figure may be Eve. The

garland, according to Eliphas Levi, represents a crown and the figure truth. It's been said it's a symbol of humanity, and the reward of a life well spent.

TEMPLES

Mountains, in all the world's religions, are places where temples are sited. In some religions the mountain itself is the temple, a cosmic place of worship. The Himalayas, Mount Etna, and Mount Fuji are representative of this sort of cosmic place of worship. *Olympus* was a word predating the Greeks that means mountains.

Some think mountains are an actual place for a gateway to Heaven. In India, at Elore and at Mamallapuram, mountains themselves were shaped into temples to Shiva.

As cities developed, mountains became less accessible. Artificial mountains called ziggurats were built – the earliest ones in Mesopotamia. The word *ziggurat* means hills of Heaven, or mountain of God.

The temple at Ankor Wat was fashioned after Mount Meru. The mountain symbolizes the whole world, so it is enclosed by a wall which represents the end of the world. A moat outside the wall symbolizes the ocean that flows beyond the end of the world. The stuppa, which is found in Ankor Wat and other South Asian temples, symbolizes a burial mount. It was thought that the architectural body replaced the dead flesh body after burial.

In Borneo, among the Dayaks, there are similar ideas. Here the village made of huts represents the universe. A steep roof is a replica of the mountain temples. The underworld is represented by the bas reliefs carved in the lowermost stones.

The mountain temples also suggested the body and its parts in the structure. The roof is shaped like the body's trunk, and the top of the mountain temple represented the skull and throat. This being was the source of all life and so he was God.

The Temple of Solomon in the Middle East possessed a cosmic dimension. The Bronze sea, incorporated at the base of the temple, symbolized the endless ocean beyond the end of the world. Egyptian temples incorporated in their designs a lake which represented the endless sea. Pillars symbolized the foundation of the earth and the support of the sky.

The architecture of the world is now divided into the religions that have the cosmic symbols and those that are based on history. Cosmic architecture can be found in Peru, China, Egypt, and India, among other countries. In the East, the mythical god was retained from the Age of Myth, and the symbolism in architecture is based on the cosmic god.

One last thought on Mountain Temples – the height of the cathedrals built in the Middle Ages suggests mountains. It may be that the mountains where temples were built influenced the height of cathedrals.

THREE

The number three is everywhere. It has connotations of magic and the sacred. Pythagoras believed that three meant the beginning, middle, and end. It became a symbol of God (the Father, Son, and Holy Ghost). And in Christianity – Faith, Hope, and Charity come in threes. There were also three wise men.

Nursery rhymes contain threes, for example "Hickory, Dickory, Dock" and the three bears.

TORTOISE

The divine tortoise presented to the Chinese wise man Lu had a scroll on its back with the numbers one through nine. Lu made this the basis for his ninefold philosophy.

The tortoise was believed to have babies from pure thought alone. It could transform itself and could create clouds from its breath. These clouds would be fogs of enchanted palaces. The tortoise was believed to live a thousand years, but when it was represented in works of art with a bushy tail, it was in its ten-thousandth year.

One of the methods of divination used by the Chinese was to read the tortoise shell. They believed the tortoise to be the holder of the secrets of life and death.

To the Egyptians the tortoise was a symbol of fecundity and long life.

The Greeks sometimes represented Venus standing on a tortoise.

Besides its attributes of the power of divination, transformation, longevity, and fecundity, the tortoise was said to carry the earth on its back. Sometimes it holds on its back the treasure mountain of the mystic jewel – the pearl. In Japanese legend it carries on its back the mountainous realm of the gods. In Hindu legend, the tortoise Akupara bears an elephant on whose back rests the world.

In prehistoric America, the legend is that the Tortoise holds the earth. The Delaware Indians believed that the Central World Tree grew out of its back. In Seneca legend, the sky mother fell into a huge pit on the wing of a tall waterfall, which placed her on a tortoise's back. In an ancient Arab myth, a whale cares for the tortoise. And it was said the earthquakes were caused by the earth tortoise waking up and yawning.

Another myth states that the female tortoise was chaos, who gave birth to the world, and was the serpent in the Garden of Eden. She is said to amuse, annoy, delight, and destroy – and is capable of evil and has endurance – and carries the world on her back.

TREE OF LIFE

The Mayans had a Tree of Life with two branches running horizontally from the top of the trunk. They symbolized a cross, and the Spanish missionaries were dumbfounded to find a cross in the new world.

Woden, the All Father, was hanged on a tree for nine days as a sacrifice. And Christ suffered death on the cross. In early Christian times there was a belief that the cross was a tree, and symbolized the Tree of Life.

The Druids used to take a dead oak tree, strip its bark, and shape it into a cross or a pillar, and continue to worship it as the symbol of the Great Spirit.

The Chinese believed the Tree of Life to be a peach tree. And it was located in the Happy Islands of the eastern ocean. The tale is that it unfurled leaves up three thousand miles high, and that a golden rooster sat in the top as the sun came up.

The Egyptians believed that the Tree of Life was a sycamore, and the gods sat on it and its fruits fed the blessed. The Tree of Osiris was a conifer. Oftentimes the people came and set it as a sacrifice and symbol of Osiris. This tree was also sacred to Dionysus. In Egypt, the most sacred of the trees was the persea – sacred to the gods because its fruit looked like hearts, and its leaves looked like tongues.

The God of the Israelites said He was like a fir tree and from Him did His people get their fruits.

The form of the conifer imitates a flame of fire, and its cone was used by the Gnostics as a sacred symbol of fire. Some think the significance of the cone derived from its phallic shape.

In parts of Europe the pear tree was sacred. Bracken was worshipped as a fire symbol, as it turned bright gold in the fall.

Arbor is the word for tree and also for fire in Latin.

In Mexico the pyramidal tree called the Yaxche is the Tree of Life. It's a perfect cone and the branches are horizontal to the trunk. It has a leafy top and its name can be translated as "great fire ever existent."

The poplar tree was sacred to Hercules, and was a symbol of the rod or spike. The laurel tree was sacred to Apollo. The rosebush was the "tree" of Eros.

Buddhists used the leaves of the Bo-tree to make a crown of honor.

The linden tree was also sacred. And the holly with the sharp twisted leaves was "holy."

TRIANGLE

This is the most complex of all symbols. It's three – one above two – and the two lower sides produce the higher as a union of positive and negative forces.

Out of this comes duality – a man's thoughts are caught in a love of his opposition, presenting a third face, which is life.

From pagan times, man has believed in a threefold universe – the divine, human, and world of nature – and that he himself was threefold – body, mind, and soul.

The triangle in primordial times symbolized the father, mother, and child. Egyptian temples were dedicated to three gods – father, mother, and child.

From the family triangle comes nature's triads – and the concept, shared by most ancient religions, of the trinity of gods.

There is magic in three, and philosophers and magicians have studied it. It is the soul of magic, astrology, and divination.

Three also stands for many. With three cheers we indicate an ad infinitum of cheers. There are groups of threes –

birth, life, and death; sun, moon, and stars; sky, earth, and water. There is a beginning, middle, and end.

Two symbolizes opposites – but three symbolizes completion.

The early Egyptians, Hindus, Druids, Mayas, and Incas believed in the three pillars – wisdom, strength, and beauty. Egyptian gods – Set, Horus, and Shu – were a primary trinity and were symbolized by a triangle inside a circle. Horus was the water, Set was drought, and Shu the god of winds and storms – the reconciler.

In Egyptian belief too, Dawn, Noon, and Sunset represented three in one, the sacred sun. Noonday was represented by Ra, sunset, Osiris, and sunrise was Horus – who was also the god of time.

Eventually Osiris, Isis, and Horus became the most powerful Egyptian gods. Osiris was the sun and Isis the moon. Osiris was identified as the son, brother, and husband of Isis. A later belief had Isis and Osiris married with Horus as their offspring. And Osiris was a bisexual Nile spirit. He represented growth, energy, and sensual power in nature. But more than anything else, Osiris was worshipped by the Egyptians as a god of triangular ability. He suffered, died, and rose from the dead to reign over the heavens.

TRIDENT

Neptune was the Roman God of the Sea, and Poseidon was his Greek counterpart. Both carried tridents. The trident is a scepter of the gods and a symbol of lightning and thunderbolts. A harpoon is similar to the trident, and Poseidon came to be known as the master of time as well as the sea.

The Trident sometimes symbolizes the third place that the sea holds after heaven and air.

TRISULA

The Trisula is a form of thunderbolt and represents the trident, the sacred tree (fleur-de-lis) and a combination of the sun disk and crescent moon. It's also a flame symbol and is the caduceus of the Indian.

It's a universal symbol and is one of the most important symbols of the ancient world, although it's so ancient its origins are lost in time.

As the Vajra – a thunderbolt – the Trisula is the scepter of diamonds of the Indian storm god. It's been compared to the discus of Vishnu and Thor's double hammer – a weapon of lightning, rain, and fertility.

The Chaldeans thought this symbol represented a trident, held by a god with an ax in his right hand. As the ax is a symbol of the sun, so the trident is a symbol of storm and water. In this god is the powerful union of fire and water.

The Vajra is, in Mesopotamia, a double trident with zigzag points to typify lightning.

In Egypt, the Trisula symbolizes the winged sun disk.

TWO PRINCIPLES

The Hindus gave the name "pair of opposites" to the dual aspects of nature which are the sun and the moon; light and darkness; heat and cold; fire and water; man and woman; day and night.

Man, since ancient times, has been symbolized by fire and by pointed objects – a spear, a column, and an arrow. Woman, the principle of water, has been symbolized by everything curving and receptive, by the earth, mountains, moon, crescent, etc.

Fire, or red, is the masculine principle – and blue is feminine, symbolically the ocean.

The sea was regarded as the mother of all things. Out of darkness and the night principle came light and life. Night was the parent of day. The Hebrew account of creation also promoted this concept. Until the spirit moved upon the face of the earth, all was chaos and darkness. The ancient races believed in a mother – or Maria – maré, the sea – and the association between woman and water was thus interpreted. Water symbolizes spirit or pure thought and matter.

Water is the cosmic element. The circle has always symbolized eternity without beginning or end. It is a symbol of water, which in turn symbolizes spiritual rebirth.

U V

Unicorns

Vessels
Virgin Mary
Vishnu
Vowels

UNICORN
The unicorn was first mentioned in 400 B.C. by a Greek doctor who said that he'd seen one in India. Powdered unicorn horn is purportedly an antidote to every kind of poison known to man. Myths about the unicorn are many: no hunter can kill it; it is untameable. If a virgin sits in the forest, the unicorn will come up to her and lay its head in her lap and go to sleep. One Christian theme said that Jesus was the unicorn and entered the Virgin's body to be borne by her. Because of this story, the unicorn became an erotic symbol. In Europe and America, the unicorn is thought by some to have healing powers. On occasion the unicorn is used as a symbol for doctors and pharmacists.

VESSELS
Mystic cups, vases, chalices, and other objects were drawn in all sizes, and the symbolism is intricate in design. The ornamentation customarily indicates what the contents are.

Upon study, Mexican and Greek pottery symbols are very similar. There is a wave pattern on the vessels of both cultures that is similar—and the wavy lines may be said to represent the dew of the Holy Spirit and the healing waters that promote salvation.

The dove of the Holy Spirit, as well as the Heart of Love, appears on some early vases.

Sometimes grapes which symbolized the new wine of Christ's Kingdom of God, adorned early vases.

Another early vessel carries the seven circles—which are the seven-fold perfection of the Holy Spirit.

VIRGIN MARY
Her many names include "Rose of Sharon" and "Cedar of Lebanon." As Queen of Heaven, she is sometimes portrayed standing on the crescent moon. On her head she wears the crown of the twelve stars of the Assumption.

Her celebratory day is March 25—"Lady Day"—a date that was earlier celebrated by the Greeks and Romans as the festival of the "Blessed Virgin Juno." Isis bore the same title as the Virgin Mary (Mother of God, Queen of Heaven)—and Isis, too, is portrayed symbolically as standing on the crescent moon with twelve stars in her crown.

Since the earliest days of Christianity, Mary has stood as a symbol of the Church and of the Christians whose salvation is Jesus.

One of the Virgin titles is Stella Maris (Star of the Sea). The same title belonged to Isis and other pagans, and was probably assimilated into the Christian Church.

The Greek God Dionysus was born of a Virgin—Myrrha—as was Hermes. The name Myrrha is related to the sea. Their purity was attributed to the cleansing of the water which purified the soul.

During the inquisition, the Art Censor made certain that all paintings of the Madonna showed her wearing a blue cape and a pure white robe and that her hair was blonde.

In the Virgin Mary's incarnation as Wisdom as depicted in one Medieval painting, she holds the sunlight in one hand and a chalice filled with dew in the other. Dew symbolizes mysticism and is thought to awaken those who sleep in the dust (of sin). In the background of the painting are wild animals trying to attack her. She survives their evil onslaught and maintains her chalice of dew so that Christians inherit her light forever.

Marigolds and lilies of the field are symbolically mystic to the Virgin Mary.

The flame is a symbol of the Virgin, and also of Isis.

The Catholic Church calls Mary the Mother of Grace, who guides us to the harbor of salvation. She is also Health of the Ills. When the mystics speak of sickness they mean mental illness. So those with emotional and psychological difficulties should send prayers of healing to the Virgin.

The Gnostics used the Seal of Solomon (see Stars) as a means of getting to the Kingdom of Light. They believed that at death the soul was brought before the Virgin (provided the mark of her seal was on it) and that thereafter that soul dwelled in the Kingdom of Light.

VISHNU

Vishnu the sun is a spiritual symbol, some say, and is a Hindu deity. He has two wives, Sarasvati and Lakshmi, symbolic of the mother goddess Mahalakshoni.

Sarasvati symbolizes beauty of the mind, and Kalshmi symbolizes outer beauty—the beauty of nature, especially.

The elephant-faced god, Ganesh, is the son of both goddesses. He represents fertility and is the god of Prosperity and successful endeavor.

There is a place in Kent, England, that has a representation of Ganesh there. In Rheims, France, there is a carved Ganesh as the lord of the gang and he's also lord of all Siva's attendants. The attendants are half divine.

The first three incarnations of Vishnu, the second person of the Hindu trinity, are the Fish, the Turtle, and the Boar.

There is an account in the Hindu literature of the fish reincarnation—with Vishnu imparting knowledge to the son of the Sun. There's a description of a huge flood and how the seeds and other items were saved by Vishnu while in his fish incarnation.

The conch shell is a symbol of Vishnu. When battle was about to be engaged, the Hindu Prince stood on the steps of a temple and gave the signal to begin by blowing on the conch shell.

The third incarnation of Vishnu was Baroha, the Boar, and he plows the land with his snout.

Vishnu holds in his hands four symbols. They are the conch shell, the disc, the mace, and a lotus flower.

Budha, the god, was the night incarnation of Vishnu. This Budha was not Buddha, the man who was a reformer. The god Budha was supposed to have written a treatise on the care of elephants and their diseases.

Budha sometimes appears as Vishnu and carries a trident as his emblem. He is symbolically the serpent or Dragon of Wisdom.

VOWELS

Letters are symbols that create an idea in the consciousness. All letters are associated with a color, and a particular sound, as well as a characteristic form. Each one is also associated with a symbolic number. Without knowledge of these symbols, we are at sea in ignorance about many of the forces that guide us.

Curved letters are female in principle, and straight lines are male. Vowels are the most useful in expression.

A: The letter A is composed of straight lines, hence it's male. It symbolizes life, power, leadership—among other attributes. The standing lines of A represent intellectual verities, and the crossbar symbolizes the unity of all things under God.

The vowel A is symbolic of one and the color red. It is life-giving and symbolizes cosmic fire. It is intellectual, requires proof like a Doubting Thomas, and it can achieve great things, or be a bust, depending on the individual it represents. If A is the first vowel in a name, it stands for sensitivity, generosity, and intuition. He's a leader, but his opposite is arrogant. When the ego is toward the criminal, he is a lying-cheating sort of fellow. If he's a powerful leader, then the intellect is all. Summer is the best season for A's as they renew their vital forces then. A comes from the Hebrew Aleph and he has the ox on his face. A tends to have diseases of the head.

E: Letter of the alphabet that represents ideas. The letter comes from an Egyptian hieroglyphic. E stands for truth, adaptability, and is a negative letter. It's the Gemini of the alphabet, denoting a war between mental and spiritual values. The material side is particularly active in E.

The second vowel, E, has the qualities of both A and I. The numbers 5 and 8 correspond to E, as does the color red. If it's more than an I in qualities, then its color is blue and its number 8. E is a person who is critical, intellectual, creative, and sensitive to the symbolism of A or I. These people can be impulsive and adaptable as well as intuitive. E's can be influenced by strong people of other symbols and can become hypnotized by them. E's are reasoners, and take it on the chin when adverse circumstances occur. They're able to help others in need unless the E is one gone bad—in which case they're unfeeling and hard. A bad E goes for the jugular. E has both female and male attributes. E's stomach, colon, and nerves are vulnerable to disease.

I: Symbols conceal meanings that are straightforward. But while sheltered from view, occult meaning is preserved. Symbolism opens up the unconscious and reveals the world to conscious scrutiny. In hieroglyphics, I is pictured as a hand. It symbolizes the thrusting forth of the hand in greeting. And it also symbolizes healing, which comes through the hand magnetically. It represents the air we breathe, height, ambition, and masters whatever it sets out to learn.

I's number is 10 and its color is blue. I's are tenacious and virile—and are hard to change once they've made up their minds. I's hieroglyphic is of a hand reaching out to others or to grasp for oneself. I's are very intense, and work and play hard. I's can also be great healers. They're passionate and strong willed. An I can easily make fun of others and also expect value for service or money. I's accumulate money and power. They ask advice and then ignore it, following their own self-will. They are easily led into alcoholism and other addictions. They're liable to diseases of the nerves and glands, and fall is their season for rejuvenation.

O: Originally symbolized by an eye. Means mental acuity. Prophecy is an attribute of O. Strong willpower, the ability to be far-sighted, and to gather what is enduring. O is self-willed and, when opposed, creates an unpleasant aura. Outbursts are common with O. These people are mean, but when they are calm, you forget the negative things they said. O's are willful and liberal. They are sensuous and irritable. They are not associated with a bad character, however, and make good friends.

Able to synthesize material into original ideas. Its colors are yellow, red, and blue, and its number is 10. It is drawn to black, as well as accidents and criticism of an unpleasant sort. O's are not easily understood, even though they know many people. They can be lonely at a crowded cocktail party. Very intuitive people are the O's. Its hieroglyphic is an eye, symbolic of mental acuity. They sometimes possess the power of prophecy. When living as good O's, these people can sacrifice much for the general good. The opposite of the good O is extreme sensitivity, irritability, willfulness, maliciousness, and viciousness. O's, when they're the good kind, have great mental power, and can be national leaders. Winter is the season for the O's renewal.

U: Represents conflict between God and man and his essences—the spiritual and the material. Denotes intellect, reason, not given to new ways of thinking. Has cheerfulness as a base and enjoys life. Strength and creativity are aspects of U.

The number of U is six, and the colors associated with it are yellow, as well as orange and brown. The characteristics associated with a name beginning in U are: self-protection, resistance, and stick-to-it-iveness. The ego determines whether U's colors are yellow, orange, or brown, or by wisdom—which is indicated by yellow. If a light color, U's are practical people. They need to be taught to be self-sacrificing and to help other people, and they are strengthened by discipline. U's don't like to ask directions or answer questions unless they can be sure they're right. They hate to display ignorance. They can attract people easily or just as easily repel them. U's are unhappy with themselves until they become spiritual.

The selfish side of a U shows when he does things just for himself. U's are noted for indecision and have trouble making up their minds. U's are likely to have diseases of the glands, blood, and liver.

W

Water
Wheel
White Horse
Wisdom

WATER

These are stories of healing waters in the folk-lore of most cultures. The quest for the water of life derives from those beliefs. Even in fairytales the water brought the beautiful princess back to life. Tales of a Fountain of Youth can also be found in the folklore of all cultures. It was once thought that such a fountain could be found in Florida or Puerto Rico. Whoever finds the water and drinks it lives forever.

WHEEL

The wheel is an ancient symbol of the sun. It is a disk with four points crossing on it. It's associated with the lotus flower—which is also a solar symbol. The lotus with eight petals is also symbolic of the eight-spoked wheel of Buddhism. These spokes symbolize the eight-fold path of self-knowledge. The wheel, to the Buddhists, is the wheel of Good Law and it turns twelve times for each of the four truths.

Buddhism is the key of the wheel which rolls over the earth. It symbolizes the doctrine of perpetual cycles of existence—reincarnation.

In India, the wheel is an important symbol, as it represented the chariot that the sun god drove across the sky. Some wheels are portrayed with four spokes, representing the four seasons, and some with twelve spokes, symbolizing the twelve months.

During the days of Veda, the wheel symbolized the occult power of the sun. It represented perfection in completion. One of Vishnu's symbols was the fiery wheel, which returns like lightning. Karma was called the wheel of fate that turns unceasingly. The sun with rays became the thousand-spoked wheel of victory.

Among the Assyrians, the solar wheel was a symbol of life, and the god that represented the wheel was one of war, but also fertility. This was the god Ashur who was the

Assyrian sun god, and he was thought to bring the seasons and animate the wheel.

Shamash, the solar deity of the Babylonians, is depicted seated on his throne with a sun wheel in front of him. The spokes create stars and had three water rays rippling outward.

Catherine wheels, in fireworks, are said to come from the pagan solar wheels.

WHITE HORSE

The color white symbolizes soul, purity of thought, and the holy life, and white horses are special in many cultures.

The historian Tacitus records that in Northern Europe, snow-white horses were raised in a sacred grove at public expense. They were never used for mundane occasions, but the King or High Priest was allowed to hitch them to their chariots. Their neighing was closely monitored, and from that the will of the gods was observed. It was thought the white horse knew the secrets of the gods.

The Druids and Persian Magi used white horses for divination, as well as the Northern Europeans. The Japanese Shintos keep three white horses in the temple of Nikko.

Among the Orientals, the white horse symbolized the sun, and in the Vedas there is a hymn to the sun as a horse.

In Wiltshire, Britain, white horses can be seen carved into the hillsides. At Bratton Hill, near Westbury, there is another white horse in the hillside.

WISDOM

The symbol for Wisdom is five circles, which in the Mayan and Egyptian symbologies, represents daylight.

Pythagoreans believed that five circles symbolized light. And for the Greeks it was a symbol for Apollo. For Freemasons the five circles stand for fellowship, or the five virtues. This all has to do with Solomon's Seal (see STARS) which has five points.

The children associated with Wisdom were the Water Mother and Hope. The Heart of Love and the Book of Knowledge were associated with them, as well as Fear in the Scales of Justice.

Knowledge and Fair Love were considered to be the main children of Wisdom.

In the symbol of the crossed keys, they are represented by two pearls or circles. The two circles appear in the Vase of Wisdom, and so became Mother Love and Knowledge symbols.

The five children of Wisdom appear as animal eyes and nostrils. When drawn as circles, they represent Perfect Love and Perfect Wisdom.

The symbolic eyes were associated with the Star of Light. Here two circles are combined with three lightrays flowing out of the mouth of a bull. The Stag had antlers like sun rays (the rising sun), and it became a solar symbol.

Griffins with eagle heads and lion bodies were known to symbolize Wisdom and Enlightenment, and their job was to oversee the god of Wisdom. They sometimes suggested Wisdom in her guise as the Water Mother.

Griffins also decorate the headpiece of Minerva, and they often also guard the Vase of Wisdom.

X Y Z

Xanthippe

Yellow
Yoni
Yoke

Zodiac

XANTHIPPE

Means "yellow horse" in English translation. She was the wife of Socrates when he married in later life. Their three children were still small when he killed himself by drinking Hemlock.

Xanthippe has been portrayed as a shrew, but some people say that Socrates' lifestyle may have caused her to be this way. In any case, Xanthippe is a modern symbol for a nagging, quarrelsome wife.

YELLOW

It's the color of the sun. It can also symbolize jealousy, malice, and treachery. It became a color of evil. Judas is portrayed in paintings wearing a yellow cloak. Yellow is also symbolic of cowardice.

YONI

This is a sanskrit word for the womb. In the Shiva cult, it's represented as a ring, or several rings, at the base of the linga, which is the phallic symbol. This appears as a short pillar. The yoni and the linga together constitute a duality—the feminine and masculine principle—without which there would have been no world creation.

The combination of the Kundalini snake—the symbol of energy—together with a yoni—represents the interconnectedness of matter.

YOKE

This is a symbol of discipline and, when represented with the ox, it means sacrifice.

ZODIAC

This is an imaginary belt that divides the heavens into the twelve constellations of the Zodiac.

Each constellation has its own symbol, usually an animal of some kind. In almost every country and age, various characteristics of the Zodiac have been expressed. It is some-times represented as a circle with twelve signs in relation to the seven planets of our solar system. There is a difference between the astrological Zodiac (the constellations) and the Zodiac of the mind (which are the symbols). The names of the constellations came from the Zodiac symbols.

BIBLIOGRAPHY

Addington, Jack Ensign. *The Hidden Mysteries of the Bible*. New York: Dodd Mead, 1969.

Aehen, Sven Tito. *Symbols Around Us*. New York: Van Nostrand Reinhold, 1978.

Agrawala, V. S. *Sparks From the Vedic Fire*. Benares: Banaras Hindu University, 1962.

Bayley, Harold. *The Lost Language of Symbolism*. New York: Barnes & Noble, 1957.

Bayley, Harold. *The Lost Language of Symbolism*. Rowan and Littlefield, 1974.

Bevan, Edwin Robert. *Symbolism and Belief*. Folecraft, Penn.: Folecraft Lebroy Editions, 1976.

Brown, Sanger. *Sex Worship and Symbolism*. Boston: Gorham Press, 1922.

Busenback, Ernest. *Symbols, Sex and the Stars in Popular Beliefs*. New York: Truett Sicker Company, 1949.

Cameron, Frederick Sillar. *The Symbolic Pig*. London: Oliver & Boyd, 1961.

Carter, Charles E. O. *Symbolic Directions in Modern Astrology*. New York: MaCoy Publishing Company, 1947.

_____. *The Dragon of the Alchemists*. London: E. Matthews, 1926.

Chaplin, Dorothea. *Matter, Myth and Spirit: Keltic and Hindu Links*. London: Rider, 1935.

Chaplin, Dorothea. *Mythological Bonds Between East and West*. Copenhagen: Einas Mungsgaard, 1938.

Cooper, J. C. *Symbolism, the Universal Language*. Wellingborough, England: Aquarian Press, 1982.

Dewey, Nellis Viola. *The Psychology of Your Name*. Chicago: Theosophical Press, 1924.

Dolgin, Janet L. *Symbolic Anthropology*. New York: Columbia University Press, 1977.

Fawcett, Thomas. *The Symbolic Language of Religion*. Minneapolis: Augsburg, 1971.

Firth, Raymond. *Symbols: Public and Private*. Ithaca, N.Y.: Cornell University Press, 1973.

Gourmont, Reny de. *The Book of Masks*. Bodeston Libraries Press, 1967.

Grombard, Ernst Hans Josef. *Symbolic Images*. New York: Praeger, 1972.

Hildebrand, Gustaf Emanuel. *The Drama and the Symbols*. Philadelphia: Farhen Press, 1970.

Lawler, James R. *The Language of French Symbolists*. Princeton, N.J.: Princeton University Press, 1969.

Nott, Charles Stanley. *An Introductory Lecture on the Symbolic Importance of Chinese Jade*. St. Augustine, Fla.: The Record Company, 1941.

Seward, Barbara. *The Symbolic Rose*. New York: Columbia University Press, 1960.

The Symbolic Animals of Christianity. London: Stuart & Watkins, 1970.